PARABOLA

PARABOLA

EXPERIENCING JESUS AS REALITY

KELLY DEPPEN

ENDORSEMENTS

Kelly Deppen's love and passion for Jesus infect the reader with a greater hunger for more of the Reality of Jesus in their life. Although the church has sometimes been guilty of 'watering down' Jesus, this book presses us to receive Him as real in both the eternal *and* physical realms. Kelly Deppen loves Jesus!

Brett Heald
Pastor, SpiritLife Church
Auckland, New Zealand

****

The Lord has directed Kelly to write *Parabola*. It vividly describes the rich, deep relationship that God has provided for us. May this book take you deeper in that relationship. God has always been after you!

Gary Yoder, President
Fresh Vision Global Ministries

****

Parabola gives a prophetic voice to basic scientific theories. But this isn't high brow, egghead stuff. Reading her book is like sitting at the table over a cup of coffee talking to a good friend. She speaks simply without over-simplifying. She is expressive and real. She doesn't pretend to be a scientist, but she is a child of God. And it is with the wonderment and heart of a child that she brings God's heart and understanding to complex things — all with the purpose of seeing and experiencing the reality of Christ.

Gael B. Hogan, Ph.D.

****

I highly recommend Kelly's book *Parabola*. It is necessary reading for those of us who have known "there is more". Kelly helps us to unravel the great mysteries of God as she presents the blueprints of a bigger design for mankind and those of us who are called to build and expand God's Kingdom here on earth. As she begins to weave both the scientific and spiritual mysteries of the universe you will find yourself not wanting to put this book down! God has gifted her with the ability not only to understand great mysteries but to explain them in a way we all can understand!

Rev. Kathleen Bailey
Serving The Lord Ministries

****

Grace and Peace to everyone reading this book! If you want your heart to be God's place to stay for the rest of your life, then you will profit from this book. Proverbs says to choose a good reputation over great riches. The LORD confides different things to different people so that we need each other to become whole. Kelly Deppen fears the LORD and her teachings have been very helpful to me and I know they will be very enriching to those who will read this book. Be blessed!

Deusdedith Kanunu
Bridges Pastor, Tabora, Tanzania - East Africa

A PLEA FOR GRACE

Thank you for purchasing and reading this word.

I pray that it will bless you far beyond your expectations.

I pray that you will hear the heartbeat of the Father
and the Testimony of Jesus Christ.

I fervently pray that your life in Christ will become
total Reality for you. I pray that every moment
of your life is divinely supernatural!

However…

Should you disagree with what is written here,
or take exception, please be free.

You see, this is not my 'theology.'
I do not have one of those —
at least I am trying to not have a theology.
That is a school of *thought about God* and a study of God.

Who needs it?

You are reading about my relationship with the Person
I love the most. So — please… much grace!

Some of this may seem 'out there' and quite unusual and not
at all common practice and I really do not apologize, OK?

I will go to any extreme to touch His heart
and show Him love.

I will say or do anything to scribe upon the hearts of men:

GOD IS LOVE!

Grace be on us all,

Kelly Deppen
August 2008
earth time

DEDICATION

I would like to dedicate this book to my father, Charles E. Kline. He is the first human being I ever loved. Forty seven years later I am still ridiculously in love with him.

Throughout school, college, marriage, and career — there was Dad — almost omnipresent. I could be in the middle of anything and there was Dad grinning from ear to ear.

It was his ever present and unconditional love and his presence in my life that at a very early age completely opened my spirit to the Love of God the Father, Jesus, and Holy Spirit. I was born into parity and I know this is due to Dad in great measure.

Dad like my Heavenly Father has never, ever disappointed me.

"Dad, I know what a heavenly gift you are. I honor you."

ACKNOWLEDGEMENTS

David Deppen — The best husband in heaven and earth. Your labor and financial support of the Kingdom of Jesus has come up for a memorial. And, I love you.

Bill and Miriam Deppen — How's the party? Your huge financial contributions to Bridges, theparabola.com, this project and the Kingdom of Jesus are only a part of the Godly inheritance you have left for us.

Mom — You pray for me every day! Every day my joy is increased through that! I love you!

Mitchell — You are the truest thing! Thanks for listening to me postulate and prophesy and for suspending all judgment. I love you!

And thanks to our friends far and wide who have extended grace and encouragement. Thank you for having eyes to see and ears to hear.

FOREWORD

I t is an honor and privilege for me to recommend to you a delightful daughter in the Lord, Kelly Deppen. Kelly is one of the new breed of the daughters of Zion who are coming of age and maturity, who are bringing a new sound from heaven's throne room. These Holy vibrations manifest themselves in dreams, visions, and prophetic words that release a Greater Reality of Jesus Christ into the earth realm. Throughout her book, "The Parabola, Experiencing Jesus Christ As A Reality" Kelly opens her spirit and heart with freedom, boldness, and clarity to impart to earnest seekers the call to live in Christ Jesus in Fullness, NOW! Not only does Kelly reveal her insatiable hunger for knowing God as Father, she also reveals a burning desire to live in Kingdom Reality. She is on a hot pursuit to discover and explore the dimensions of parity with heaven. Her love for Jesus is contagious. Kelly shares many heavenly experiences with us that define her quest to walk and live in the Eleventh Dimension that represents the time period just before Jesus' rule is established in the earth realm. I believe all who study this revelatory word with an open heart and spirit will benefit greatly as I have. Through the eyes of Jesus, Kelly has experienced a High Covenant Reality. She has discovered the supernatural Jesus. He has become the love of her life. This is the true reality of heaven and earth. Kelly's revelation has distinguished her as a trail blazer and forerunner that takes us through Christ's precious blood to embrace Him as the True Parabolic Prophet. She too, has that parabolic anointing upon her life. May we all drink from this cup and receive an impartation of the present day truth.

Jerry Phillips
Jerry Phillips Ministries

ONE THING REALITY

J esus the Christ is All-in-All. We say that a lot. It sounds really good because it makes Him the focus, and that is as it should be. He is the only focus worth focusing on.

There is so much more. Saying that He is All-in-All reveals Him as the multi-dimensional God, One who is so vast and so unsearchable that we lose ourselves in Him.

My hope is that reading this is a revelatory experience, that it reveals and opens up another dimension: **Christ as Reality.** My prayer is that all who read this will enter in to an entirely new reality, an entirely different mode of all life experience, spiritual, physical, mental, emotional, and relational. This is beyond the paradigm shifts and mindset changes that we've been moving in. This is messing with your reality and the very ways that you perceive everything. My sincere prayer is that you will enter into a totally new realm and reality as a human being: it is called **"in Christ Jesus."**

If you have entered into relationship with Jesus Christ of Nazareth, you are by rights and in truth "in Christ." This mystery occurs and is possible because Jesus shed His Holy Blood. Without His spilt blood we are nowhere. We are citizens of nowhere, aliens without Christ.

*"But now in Christ Jesus ye who sometimes were far off are
made nigh by the blood of Christ."*
Ephesians 2:13

The Holy Blood brings us *in.* Jesus' blood brought us into
salvation and redemption and the new covenant with God.
His blood brought us into **the holiest.** Ephesians says we were
"brought nigh." The Greek for *nigh* means near, it also means
into place or position. That positioning is the nexus of the
earthly and the heavenly. It is the Darling of heaven come into
the earth realm, Jesus of Nazareth. Paul goes on to say in this
chapter of Ephesians that essentially we are brought so close
to God by the blood of His Son that if we reach out and grope
around we will touch God.

We are to be confident and bold and assured of our ad-
mittance to the Holy Place.

*"Having therefore, brethren, boldness to enter
into the holiest by the blood of Jesus,"*
Hebrews 10:19

However, your current *experience and perception* may not
be congruent with those facts. Perhaps you are experiencing Christ at times, and something called warfare at others.
Maybe your world and your life is a collection of little compartments: home, work, church, leisure, and so on. And as you
experience each separate little box of life you have varying
degrees of Christ-consciousness. The frustration comes as we
take inventory of our lives and see that in some areas we have
a strong and powerful and transcendent awareness of Christ,
and in others we are seriously lacking, and this we like to call
"the flesh."

So, what to do? Current theology and teaching and a great
deal of inspirational writing would have us all study harder,

devote more time, attend more church, memorize more scripture, fast, plead with God in prayer, roll over and bark at the moon. We are taught and encouraged to go through all of these machinations in order to get more of Jesus into all of our compartments, essentially to stuff as much of Jesus as we can into our little boxes. The Lord of Glory, the ever-expanding Christ cannot be contained or compartmentalized.

I tried. I promise I did. I had a plan to get Jesus into every area of my life. It looked like an elegant strategy. I had specific tactics for each area of my life. Every year I took the week between Christmas and New Years and I fasted and prayed and believed that I sought the Lord on the plan and strategy for the upcoming year and that this was going to be the year that I got all of my little life compartments all filled up with Jesus. I *assumed* that this would make Him very happy. He is so infinitely patient.

Then, one beautiful summer day, I heard from Him regarding my strategy. And guess what, He hated it. It angered Him!

As I was out on a three mile walk in the country, Jesus revealed Himself to me, stopped me in my tracks along a country road and told me in no uncertain terms that He would never leave me or forsake me, but that day *He quit my company*. He in His mercy said, "Take this program and shove it. I am not going to work here anymore." It gets better. He said, "I am done relating to you in your terms, through the maze of this life strategy that you have, in your narrowly prescribed way of operating, in your career-minded and religious counterfeit realm." Those He loves He chastens.

In small part I understand why Paul was blind for three days after he was messed up by Jesus on the Damascus road. After hearing His words I fell to my knees on the side of the road and wailed as I watched this house of cards that I called my life utterly collapse. As I sat in the grass by the side of the road in a snotty heap, I saw the construct of my life as a heap of rubble. There were not even any shards of my life worth picking up again. I saw the pile of filthy rags and it was me.

There stood Jesus. He looked peaceful. His face was open and restful. He stood beside me quietly. He had nowhere else to be and all of the time in the world. He was not concerned or disturbed, He just was.

I began to cry aloud from my spirit, "I am so sorry Lord!" Over and over this repentance came from deep places within me. You know, I was sorry for what I had done and the way I was living, but I was most sorry for how I made Him feel. I had frustrated Him and tried to direct and contain Him according to my finite and flawed ideas. I had come to Him over and over again for Him to bless and grace my programs and ambitions and my church's programs. He felt used.

Then, a smile broke out on His face and His big brown eyes got squinty at the corners as He beamed down at me. I looked up into the face of forgiveness. He is beautiful. He extended His big paw of a hand to me and helped me up. And, as I was wiping my nose on the sleeve of my tee shirt, we took the first steps with Him in the lead. He began to impart to me His vision and plan and purpose for my life, my destiny in Him, my path, my purpose, my focus, the object of my affections: **Him.**

This was a new day. The beginning of days. I was a new creature. My life and I had gloriously disappeared, and I was reduced to one thing: *one who beholds Him.* My plans? I no longer had any. What would I do? Whatever He was doing. What about the roles that I fulfilled in life, the titles that I walked in? Gone forever. Then, what do I do, and who am I?

A woman in love.

"One thing have I desired of the Lord, that will I seek after, that I may dwell in the house of the Lord all the days of my life, to behold the beauty of the Lord, and to enquire in His temple."
Psalm 27:4

This is my heart as a lover of the Lord. The lover in the psalm is focused on the beautiful beloved. It is an intense focus that has led into such intimacy that he enjoys an open invitation to enquire in the temple of God. This is imperative for all of us.

God desires to speak to us *openly*. Like with Jacob and Moses and Abraham, He desires to speak face- to- face. This openness is *parrhesia* in Greek. It means open, frank and unreserved. It means boldly, plainly, fearlessly and conspicuously. This is the relationship Christ's blood makes possible.

Parrhesia is also the Greek vernacular for 'freedom of speech.' No first amendment is necessary in heaven or in our relationship with God. We are entirely free to speak our minds. *Parrhesia* also connotes fullness. The first time the word is used in the New Testament is in Mark chapter eight. This is where Jesus tells His disciples of His imminent crucifixion.

*"And he began to teach them, that the Son of man must suffer many things, and be rejected of the elders, and [of] the chief priests, and scribes, and be killed, and after three days rise again. And he spake that saying **openly**. And Peter took him, and began to rebuke him."*
Mark 8: 31-32

Jesus proclaimed His coming death with confidence and boldness and without mincing words. The very event He was proclaiming, the shedding of His innocent blood, is the act that gives us liberty in heavenly places and complete freedom to approach the Throne.

His life blood opened the sanctuary for us and allows us into the Holiest place. The door to the House of God stands wide open to us. Christ is that door and we must pass through into experiencing heaven as reality and *Christ as Reality*. Heaven is the seat of life for us. We are seated in heavenly places *in Christ Jesus*.

Look at the *location* of this focused worship and behold-ing and dialoging. The psalmist desires to *dwell in the House of the Lord* all the days of His life. Where is this place and how do we get there?

The House of the Lord, is this a conceptual place like uto-pia or something mythical? Is it a building called a church? I don't think so. Of course on one level this place is the third heaven which is the literal, physical dwelling place of the Fa-ther, the Lord Jesus, the heavenly host and the great cloud of witnesses. It is both a spiritual place and reality as well as a physical place and physical reality. God can do two things at once.

Another dimension of the reality of the House of the Lord is that you and I *are* the house of the Lord because He has come to dwell in us and we have been inhabited by His Spirit. We say that He has come to make His home in our hearts and we acknowledge that we are the living temple of God.

On yet another, higher dimension, Jesus Himself is the House of the Lord. Jesus entered the physical realm and dwelt among us in flesh. He has totally human flesh that houses total and absolute Divinity. He is not simply a divine person, He is **Divine Reality**. Jesus Christ constitutes and defines the reality for His people, those who define them-selves as being **in Christ**. The construct of this divine real-ity can be viewed as being the house or habitation of the Lord.

So, being **in Christ** not only means belonging to Him and being a member of the Body, to be **in Christ** also establishes our **location.**

"For in Him we live, and move, and have our being; as certain also of your poets have said, for we are also His offspring."
Acts 17:28

The apostle Paul went toe-to-toe with the intellectuals in Athens at the famous University of Greece. He did not address the "polite and refined idolaters and heathens" as Matthew Henry called them, on matters of theology alone. Paul appealed to their intellectual need to understand *cosmology*, and the very **Nature of Reality.** He understood that these were people whose lives were devoted to grasping R**eality.**

The mathematicians, astronomers, physicists and poets who gathered at Mars Hill must have been stirred up by the way that Paul addressed the very concepts that they held so dear. Paul led them to perceive the connection between the question of the nature of reality that was their consuming passion, and the *"unknown God of Moses,"* to whom they had built an altar.

Paul's lecture gave them a window into a truth that they passionately pursued scientists, mathematicians and poets alike. This is the fact that the physical realm is co-inhabited with another unseen realm or dimension, namely that of the spirit. This spirit realm and higher dimension interleaves the physical world. All of their theories and hypotheses, all of the inspiration of their poets testified the existence of this ethereal place.

Then Paul hit them with a big fat whammy, these people who gathered and spent all of their time in pursuit of some new thing: This unknown God they ignorantly worshipped: HE IS REALITY. He is the *highest attainable reality.*

In Him 'being' happens. In Him we move about and we *are.* The fullness of LIFE is in Him. Outside and apart from Him is a linear, futile, earth-bound existence: a sad trip through time and space that always and without exception leads to death.

The name of this realm, this wasteland, is *mortality.* It is the prison camp of the unenlightened. This is a realm where even birth is seen as the first step toward death. Here you are born; you work, and then die. Life here is flat because it is two-dimensional. You occupy space and you are in the chain gang called time. Since there is no vision here into the other realms, people perish.

There is another realm where life happens. This is the physical world which Christ permeated and changed. He came and literally split time. Any physicist will tell you that time cannot be affected without space being altered. Time and space are the twin coordinates of physical reality. Time and space are the tent and tent posts of the construct we call the time-space continuum.

So at the same moment Christ split time in two, or B.C. and A.D., He created a new realm and a new dimension called "in Him." This is simultaneously a seen and an unseen realm. I am "in Him" as I sit on this chair at this computer and write these words. I am "in Him" and He is in me as I am participating in His Spirit and as His Spirit inspires the writing of these words.

Since His resurrection Jesus has pursued one thing, the edict of the Father to gather all things into Himself.

"Having made known unto us the mystery of his will, according to his good pleasure which he hath purposed in himself: That in the dispensation of the fullness of times he might gather together in one all things in Christ, both which are in heaven, and which are on earth; [even] in him."
Ephesians 1:9-10

If you really study Paul's words here a few things become clear. First, He is delighted to bring us into Himself. This isn't some task or chore to Him; this is what causes Him pleasure because this is the mysterious and perfectly loving will of our Heavenly Father. I am thankful that Jesus is Reality and not simply religion.

Secondly, if you delve into this passage in the original language you learn that 'the fullness of times' is not just some far off date that God is keeping secret. We are not just sitting here in the earth realm waiting for the celestial clock to chime twelve bells or something. We humans are so linear and detached in our thinking. Fullness of times is the *kairos* moment. It is the opportune time when things have come to a desired and specified state. You and I are those things, and we are much more participants in the determination of 'the fullness of times' than we have ever imagined.

I believe that we will see the dynamic shifts and changes in the Body of Christ and therefore in the world when we embrace the *Reality of Life in Christ*, and when we submit to Jesus as the determinate of our individual and corporate reality. In other words, everything will shake loose for the return of Christ when we awaken to Him as our Truth, our Fact, our Reality, and our All-in-All. When we move all of our experience of physical and spiritual reality into Jesus, we will have come into a second chapter of Acts unity that is irresistible to Him.

We need wildly expanded perception and discernment. We need to be fully awakened to this higher reality and we need to vigorously exercise our senses to experience all of Him. I know that even as I write these words, the Apostle Paul, and a great cloud of witnesses paces in intercession for us. They pray that we will awaken to the height and depth and length and breadth, the full dimensionality of our lives in Christ. This is the hope of Kingdom progress and growth. We need a new reality as a being living and existing in a realm of God and heaven called 'in Christ Jesus.' We must have awareness of this wonderful and mysterious truth.

Do you suppose that Paul's Pooh-Bahs back in Athens got the concept? Perhaps some did because the word says that there were a few conversions. Those converted were enlightened. Still, there were probably those who missed the point because they were offended in their intellectual or theological sensibilities.

What is our excuse for missing the point, or, what has caused us to miss the point? In a word: religion, man-made two-dimensional doctrine that has kept the church trapped inside of time and earth-bound. Religion always reduces a transcendent and living Truth to an aphorism. In other words, religion takes Truth and *flattens it* into just two dimensions, taking the life and the eternity and the spirit out of it.

Modern day believers quote Acts 17:28 as a mantra of membership in the Body of Christ.

"For in him we live, and move, and have our being; as certain also of your own poets have said, For we are also his offspring."

There is so very much more to God and His Truth. We must open ourselves up to Him to receive the **fullness** of Who He is and that fullness contains the higher Truth that **He desires to BE our Reality.**

This fullness that His death bought means embracing the higher truth that we are **eternal spirit beings,** and we are for a moment also experiencing time, space, and the physical dimension. We have to reframe and refocus the entire way in which we experience existence. We have to come into the revelation that corporal reality is temporary and that it co-exists with life in the Spirit, which is eternal.

For too long we have lived as earth-bound captives of religion. It is for freedom that He set us free. This means that you are free to make the break from the bonds of earth and from the restriction of experiencing only physicality. You are free to be fully **real.**

Read Acts 17:28 again

"For in him we live, and move, and have our being; as certain also of your own poets have said, For we are also his offspring."

He is telling us that in addition to being the personage of God the Savior and God the Son:

He is our location.

He is the locality of our lives.

He is home.

He is our atmosphere and our environment in which we live.

We move in Him, therefore, wherever we are, that place is called Jesus.

We have our being in Him. Our awareness of our existence does not happen apart from Him.

In this season, He has the doors of heaven and the windows of revelation open to us, that we may receive this fresh revelation and allow it to carry us from *glory to glory*. Jesus, the King of Glory is knocking on every door in this hour. He is asking that we allow Him to enter in and that we too enter into a greater revelation and manifestation of Him.

He desires to come in and sup with us.

Do you desire that as well?

Doesn't that presuppose that we are in the *same place and time as He is?* We must stop reducing the Word of God to one-dimensional sayings. We must take Him at his word and allow the Word of God and the Son of God to become alive in us.

This is spiritual growth: to grow in the knowledge of Him and the revelation that there are limitless dimensions to God and His Spirit, and these revelations are all open to us and they are all for us. Regrettably, religion and tradition and superstition have stolen higher reality from us, aborting this growth. We've been smashed and flattened and stuffed into a box comprised of the physical realm and our physical experience, what some like to call "the world." Then, on top of this boxed up existence and pre-packaged religion, we have been infected by a deadly religious virus called *fear*.

Many are gripped by the fear of actually having a true spiritual experience in God. "What would He think?"

I promise you, He will be thrilled!

CHAPTER TWO

WHAT IS A FLIPPIN' PARABOLA?

T his is the tale of how I came to Christ as Reality. It is a bit loopy so hang on for the ride. God gives us revelation whenever and however He sees fit. In other words, you can't make this stuff up.

The Shift

Several years ago I attended a prophetic conference, where there was a powerful prophetic convergence occurring. There was an open heaven from the beginning of worship on the first night. A well-known prophetic guy was speaking. He was sharing his life experiences and the many ways that God had delivered him and given him authority in various areas.

This man stated that he believed himself to be a **parabolic prophet**. He meant that his experiences, visitations, rhema words and so on are used by God as *parables* or examples of seasons or circumstances that others and perhaps the church would experience. God had given him a foretaste or foreknowledge to minister to this. He meant that in these things he was having a first-fruits experience.

As he spoke the words "parabolic prophet" I was hit with lightening from Heaven. The lightening hit me in the mid-section and threw me back in my seat. My friends sitting around me thought I was throwing some sort of spasm because nothing else seemed to be going on.

Since the words being spoken were teaching and not prophecy or ministry, the atmosphere in the place was normal for the most part. And then there was me. I sat bolt upright, eyes bulging, shaking under the power of God. I was barely able to draw a breath, and I was beginning to weep. I think it occurred to my friends at this point to get me some ministry after the service for emotional issues or bad behavior.

As the speaker continued to teach he once again used the terminology **parabolic prophet.**

Once again lightening from God hit me in the solar plexus and a groan came up out of my spirit. The trembling increased and I was now crying buckets of tears and sobbing. I could see my friends looking around for other seats to move to, but none were available. I would have excused myself and gone to the ladies room, but God had me tethered to my seat with eyes fixed on the speaker. I was His prisoner.

At this point my spirit was so hungry and curious and open to know what God was telling me, that apparently He was not telling anyone else. At the same time my mind was looking for an emotional cause to my behavior and also a way of escape.

I was in two places at once. In the physical I was freaking out over my own behavior and the fact that I seem to have no control over it. In the spirit I was completely in the Presence of God; just having been given some kind of 'pay attention' injection of lightning bolts. The one place I *was not* present and accounted for was in the conference. I had become totally oblivious to my surroundings, my friends, and the speaker. I had arrived at a new place, an alternate plane of existence, a place I like to call "out there."

As the conference continued to go on around me, speaker speaking, people chuckling, notes being taken, people sneezing—I see a cloud descend over the entire gathering. The glory of God settled in below the ceiling and above the heads of all of the people. My spirit and mind remained hyper alert and my entire body relaxed in the Presence of God. I breathed in the Glory. I drank in the Glory. I was totally wasted on the Glory. At this point I ceased to care that everyone around me was not sharing this experience. It was incredibly pleasant. I recall making a conscious decision to stay here and forget about everyone else.

Then, like a train coming through a tunnel, the words of the speaker came through the Glory cloud into me again, ".....blah, blah, blah, blah... *parabolic prophet.*"

And, I heard the audible voice of God,

"He has no idea what he is saying," said the Father.

"What do You mean?" I asked.

"I mean right now, he does not have complete revelation of the Truth and power and impact of his words." said God.

Being quite awe-struck and literally out of it, I had the crazy idea to say to the Father of Creation, "*What words?*"

"Parabolic prophet," He thundered.

My visitation with God waned and I found myself once again completely present in the meeting, looking quite messed up from my encounter and in need of a nose-blowing and face washing. I pulled it together and left the meeting as it concluded for the night. Several friends did ask if I was OK to drive and I recall mumbling at them about being 'out of season' or something and I left.

Over the next month, I was completely gripped by the words and concepts: *parable, parabolic, parabola.* I read and re-read all of the parables of Christ thinking surely God is telling me something. I thought certainly there was something I missed that I desperately needed in order to continue living. Perhaps I had a character issue that one of these parables would straighten out.

In my obsession, I developed a fervor in seeking the instruction of the Lord and Holy Spirit. I quit doing much else other than praying, contemplating my encounter, asking Him for knowledge and revelation. I began taking long hikes in the surrounding forests and going up into the mountains to be alone with God. Already, He had changed me with a word.

It is as if my literal location changed and I was now living in another realm, a realm of His Presence where physical reality was a very distant, secondary experience. Every so often, he would bring my attention to something in nature in order to show me something or teach me on a point, but for the most part I was somewhere else. And, I had no intentions of ever leaving.

Since I had ended a twenty year corporate career to do ministry full time, I had entire days to devote to Him. In the mornings I worshipped and prayed. I approached the written word like treasure and I searched it and found that memorizing had become very easy. The remainder of the day He imparted Himself to me.

Gently and steadily, the Lord began to open my eyes and understanding to what He wanted to reveal. One summer day I was taking my mom to her oncology appointment. I packed a tote full of reading materials and my journal, knowing that these appointments can be long. On the way to the appointment I grabbed the mail and saw that I had received a newsletter, so I tucked that in the tote with everything else and headed for Mom's.

We arrived at the doctor's office and I remember thinking to myself that there must have been a senior citizen special that day because the waiting room was packed with older folks. I got comfortable on a sofa and Mom got called into an exam room. I felt around in the tote bag and pulled out the newsletter. I began reading an article on spiritual eyes and ears. It was as if Holy Spirit was reading this article to me. It was so parallel to the way I had been experiencing God over the past year. I began to wipe away tears as I read the article.

There I sat in the waiting room, surrounded by seniors, weeping, and hearing Holy Spirit as clear as a bell. Then, I read the words, "…*may the Lord impart to you His spirit of wisdom and revelation…*" and Holy Spirit said to me:

"If you will kneel down right now, right here in this room, I will give you a double portion of this!"

Invitations don't get much better than that! I don't recall even thinking about it for a split second. I slid out of my seat and onto my knees and turned to face the back of the sofa. I prayed "Yes!" and I received and released His promises. When I got up from my knees, wiping my eyes, I saw that the senior citizens had rearranged themselves, and they were now all sitting on the opposite sides of the room, despite the crowded conditions. I got comfortable again and I could hear the Lord chuckling at me, at my moment of obedience that more or less cleared the room. So, I began to laugh along with Him, because frankly it was really awesome and really funny at the same time. Remarkably, my mother still lets me take her to her appointments.

After this incredible season of revelation, training and focusing, practically everything about life and the way I perceived and experienced it was different. God was reality and everything else was, well, everything else. Stuff. Matter. Temporal. Non-eternal. Not inconsequential or irrelevant, but of far lesser importance. In terms of the way in which I experienced and perceived life, the things of the earth had become strangely dim. Ironically, even my own opinions had become trivial to me, to the delight of my family and friends

What God was Really Saying

During this exquisite wilderness intimacy and instruction, God began talking to little old me about two topics that were on His Mind: science and math.

"Jesus, help me, You have the wrong girl!" How could God make such a glaring mistake?

Again, Holy Spirit talked to me about parables, parabolic, and parabolas. He is the ultimate teacher. He has a way with words, you could say, because He can take the very thoughts of the Creator of the Universe and whisper them to you, and you get it. That is miraculous! And He does this all in a setting of His own perfect patience and intimacy. He is the rabbi, you the student, the Word is the course of study and in these times nothing else exists. God, the holy trinity, and you: the perfect teacher to student ratio.

And Now...Parabolas...

Lesson one was about parabolas. Everything that I knew about a parabola you could put on the head of a pin. A parabola is a curve, ta da.

He corrected me. A parabola is a curve, yes, and it is the *expression of numbers* that *appears as a curve*. It is the **seen** manifestation of **unseen** numerical values. Remember those little graph charting exercises we all did in elementary math? Put a dot on the chart with your number two pencil in the place that corresponds to plus one and negative one, that corresponds to negative thirty-three and positive thirty-three? If you did it all correctly you got a graceful curve on both the positive and the negative sides of the graph. Sometimes the teacher had something plotted that came out looking like something fun like Mickey Mouse. You remember.

God was talking to me about these curvy little graph-thingies, and I was captivated. Suddenly, everywhere I looked these crazy curves and shapes were popping up. I realized that my satellite dish that never really produced very good TV, is a parabola. Awesome. I noticed that those curved silver observation mirrors that are up in the corners of convenience stores were parabolas. (Never, never look at yourself in one of these mirrors. Once you have seen your rear expanded to look as big as a barn you never really recover.) Everywhere I looked I saw this curved expression, and new dialogue with God ensued.

Did you know that all bridges are parabolas? Yep. Even bridges that do not look curved are in fact curved. The curves inherent in the engineering are the very thing that supports the weight of the bridge and the traffic on it. Suspension bridges are beautiful parabolas. The distribution of the weight on the curved cables is what makes the whole thing work. God clued me in to this as I was crossing the George Washington into New York City to a speaking engagement. It was an 'aha' moment.

Do you remember the Richard Dreyfus character in the movie "Close Encounters of the Third Kind"? He had a fascination with a land form which he kept seeing everywhere, such as in his mashed potatoes. Well, it was a bit like that with me and the parabolas.

CHAPTER THREE

"PLEASE HELP ME.
MY JESUS-FISH IS MISSING!"

During this time I needed some new journals and I stopped by a bookstore. After paying for the books I noticed a twirling rack that held all sorts of Christian paraphernalia. We have that you know, paraphernalia. There on the rack were magnets for your fridge and your car, you know—Jesus-fish. I have never personally owned a Jesus-fish. Anyway, I was *enthralled* with these little gizmos. I stood there agape just absorbed in the moment and the fact that the Jesus-fish happens to be two interlocked *parabolas!* Knowing that the ichthys is an ancient symbol related to first century Christianity I decided to do some historical research.

The parabolic symbol was probably used by early Christians in communicating meeting times and locations, but the origins of the symbol are not entirely Christian. The symbol once known as the **vesica pisces** was used prior to Christianity to express the cosmological idea of the place where heaven and earth intersect. (Think about two circles intersecting for a moment, in geometry this place of overlap is called a sub-set.) It depicts the overlap of the divine and the human, the shared space of the spirit and matter.

I was beginning to have a fresh appreciation for the Jesus-fish. *Jesus is the intersection of heaven and earth!* He is at once divine and human, spirit and matter. "Lord, this is deep!" I told Him.

"That's Me, unsearchable." He replied.

A parabola is the multi-dimensional expression of a mathematical equation. An equation is a mathematical expression with two sides, and they are equal to each other and both true. "So, God, what are you saying here?"

Two Worlds Colliding

"Your life in Christ in the earth is the simultaneous expression of two dimensions: matter and spirit. Flesh and spirit. Earth and Heaven. Temporal and Eternal," He said.

Now my eyes were open to the fact that **Jesus is Parabolic**. Jesus is the perfect parabolic expression of the Father. The Lord said it best Himself.

"…if you have seen the Son you have seen the Father." (John 14:9) Jesus is the human expression of the divine, fully human and fully divine. Jesus is the earthly expression of heaven and the ways of heaven. He is the living, intersecting dimensions of heaven and earth Who came to create and establish a reality where they can co-exist and glorify the Father. This territory is called **The Kingdom of God. And He is the King.**

This is our intended home on earth, this parabolic place of heaven on earth. We have been living in some darkened room or something! Religion turned the lights out and shut us all up in a box. I don't know about you but I am going to live in this Kingdom, in this reality, in Him.

"And he said unto them, When ye pray, say, Our Father which art in heaven, Hallowed be thy name. Thy kingdom come. Thy will be done, as in heaven, so in earth."
Matthew 6:10 red letters

Jesus taught us one prayer. One. In this, the ultimate prayer, he says that we are to pray the Father's will into being. What is that? That earth be like heaven, a reflection of heaven. That earth is *heavenly*. He also intends that we have an awareness and experience of heaven here in the earth realm. Jesus has opened the door to heaven as He is the Door to the Father. Go through the Door!

Jesus said it over and over, "*...the Kingdom of God **is like...**"* These are called **the parables,** *'cause* they're **parabolic!** They are word pictures, images of what the Kingdom of heaven on earth is supposed to be like. This Kingdom come to earth should look like a mirror image of as it is in heaven.

This is our intended earthly home, the area of overlap where heaven permeates earth and the government of heaven. The will of the Father *is the government*. This overlapping area of the earthly and the divine is the territory that we are to occupy and expand. However, we cannot affect a change in the earth and cause expansion *until we occupy*. We must first live here ourselves before we can expand our borders. We must begin to function in **Kingdom Reality.**

Let me ask you a question: Where do you live? No doubt you just thought of the numbers and street name where your home is located. Naturally, you know the address. You can't get there without knowing where it is. Likewise, we have to grasp the higher reality of our address, and the fact is that we live **in Christ Jesus**. This is the intended geographical location and our intended reality.

Until we have our consciousness/reality and our coordinates established we can forget about occupying and possessing the land, let alone implementing plans for expansion.

So, where are you right now? Are you in Christ Jesus?

Is this just a club like the Junior League, or is it as literal as the scriptures say?

If you are in Christ Jesus, and live and move and have your being in Him, you are where He is. I love it here.

Jesus is in heavenly places. Jesus is in the Body of Christ in the earth realm.

"Do you mean to tell me that, contrary to what I have been telling my son, I can be in two places at the same time, Lord?"

"Yep."

Contemplative Exercise

1. Ask Holy Spirit to illuminate one specific area of your Christian experience that is divided into two separate realities. See this through His eyes knowing that from this vantage point there is no condemnation—only perfect love!

2. Allow yourself to become aware of the feelings and emotions that are produced by this double-minded aspect of your experience. Since you are doing this 'in Him' remember, there can be no rejection or judgment—only grace!

3. Now, ask Him to give you a vision of His Truth for this aspect of your life. Stay quiet in this moment as Holy Spirit ministers this revelation to you. Be willing to wait upon the Lord.

4. Now express your sovereign will to relinquish the lesser, fallen reality and express your choice of Christ as

Reality in this realm. Remember that every knee must bow to the authority of Christ! Rename this land "the Kingdom of Jesus Christ" because this is now territory that belongs to Him and exists in Him. This parcel of ground has been brought into the Kingdom for such a time as this.

5. Exercise your new-creature awareness in this place. Occupy this Kingdom land. Ask for a fresh anointing of grace to focus on Him alone and the Reality of Him.

CHAPTER FOUR

IN TWO PLACES AT ONCE

We probably owe God a really big apology. We have portrayed Him as an absentee Father Who makes His adoptive children live at sleep away camp. Father, forgive us! We have behaved badly and said worse. No wonder no one wants to come and join our Kingdom, we act as if it is a Siberian outpost we want sprung from. Or we've taken on the mindset of nuisance children who have been packed off to boarding school; when we learn these lessons we get to come home to stay.

Have you ever been the unwitting victim of a religious person sharing their theology with you? It goes something like this…"Well, you know, we are just here on this earth to learn the lessons that God has for us to learn. We are getting ready for heaven." Words to that effect. What ever happened to the Holy Spirit being our teacher and our guide? Lord, can we start kicking these people in the shins? I guess not.

Where did this rejection and outcast mentality come from? Religion. Religious doctrine. False humility which is pride in our own lowliness. We seriously need a revelation of the Goodness of God and His wonderful intentions for us at all times.

> *"For I know the thoughts that I think toward you, saith the LORD, thoughts of peace, and not of evil, to give you an expected end."*
> Jeremiah 29:11 KJV

God says, "Look, I am fully aware of the thoughts, feelings, plans and strategies I have in place for you now and always. I esteem you so much more than you can even imagine. You should see the awesome stuff I have on the forecast for you!" Like the contemporary believers, Israel had gone into worldly captivity, and God says to them, "Look this was not My design! You guys started looking at Babylonians, then you started thinking like Babylonians, the next thing you know—captives!" So, we, people with the benefit of their experience, should choose to *not go there!*

> *"And ye shall seek me, and find [me], when ye shall search for me with all your heart."*
> Jeremiah 29:13 KJV

This is a heart issue and the Kingdom is a place that is first established in men's hearts. We have looked at the world and it has fascinated us, God forgive us. Have you noticed how we have tried to incorporate the flash and dash and hoopla of the world system into our church settings? For example, when did they tear down the altars and put up stages? It had to have been sometime within the last forty years. From the perspective of being in 'the audience' I have to tell you I hate it. Rock stars perform on stages. The Lord of Glory is no performer. He is to be *worshipped* in a place of His own designation called the Holy of Holies. No stage there. No performance. No flesh will glory in His Presence. I think that maybe that's why the altars used to be there, as a barrier. You approach an altar and you have a quick decision to make: kneel or leave. Humble yourself as you approach the Throne of Grace. Assume the position.

It is a heart issue. Who do we desire to *see* during worship? *Who* is the focus? The worship leaders? As Jeremiah said, when our whole hearts are beholding **Him**, we will awaken to the **reality** that He is in our midst and we are *in Him*.

> *"One [thing] have I desired of the LORD, that will I seek after; that I may dwell in the house of the LORD all the days of my life, to behold the beauty of the LORD, and to enquire in his temple."*
> Psalm 27:4 KJV

The House *of the Lord* is His temple which was in the old covenant a *physical place* where only the Levitical priests could go. Because of Jesus, we are now His temples which are at once *physical and metaphysical places*. We are the natural and supernatural temples of God. God indwells us as God the Holy Spirit. He animates us as He has breathed His *pneuma*, His very breath, into us. Metaphysically, we are *in Him* as we are all one in the Spirit.

> *"But he that is joined unto the Lord is **one spirit**."*
> First Corinthians 6:17

> *"For by **one Spirit** are we all baptized into **one** body, whether [we be] Jews or Gentiles, whether [we be] bond or free; and have been all made to drink into **one Spirit**."*
> First Corinthians 12:13

We are all immersed into one Spirit and we are overwhelmed by Him. It is like this: We have drunk of Him, and He is in us. We have breathed Him, taking Him into our being, and He is in us. We are immersed in Him, we are swimming in Him. We are afloat in Him and we are cleansed by Him. **This is communion.**

This is the place to be, a place where I can not discern where He ends or begins, where I am utterly lost in Him.

Paul prayed this apostolic prayer over the Ephesians and essentially over all of us:

"That you may be able to comprehend with all saints what [is] the breadth, and length, and depth, and height; And to know the love of Christ, which passeth knowledge, that ye might be filled with all the fulness of God."
Ephesians 3:18-19

What I think is particularly cool is that Paul writes about *the dimensions of* Jesus, God's love! Breadth, length, depth, and height. Think of a cube rather than a two-dimensional square. Think of an orb rather than a one-dimensional circle. This fully dimensional representation shows a multi-dimensional Jesus Who truly is All in All. This is exceeding abundantly above all religion and doctrine has taught us before. This is a transcendent, omnipresent, and omniscient God.

This is our **locality** in the earth realm. We are in Him and He is in us. In this place called Jesus, we are at once on earth and seated in heavenly places. We exist simultaneously in two realms.

CHAPTER FIVE

COSMIC CHRISTIANS

I have come to enjoy *cosmology,* the study of the origin of, current state of, and outlook for our universe. I am also into physics, mathematics, quantum theory and that sort of stuff. A funny thing happened two weeks ago. I was re-ferred to a new neurologist for some possible new treatment. This man, Indian by birth, was lovely, a total gentleman with impeccable manners. He was so kind and polite that he asked me what kind of work I did. I explained to him that I am a per-son who does revelatory or prophetic ministry. For a moment he looked very puzzled, and said, "Like ESP and such?"

"Well, no not really," I said. "Right now I am writing a book on Jesus Christ as the nature of reality. It illuminates the truths of Christ and the nature of cosmology, and the way they are connected." I explained.

The nurse entered the room to take my blood pressure. The doctor said to her, "Mrs. Deppen is writing a book about Jesus as a nature cosmetologist."

Lord, I knew this thing had a great potential to be misunderstood. However, the doctor did request a copy of the book.

So, here's the thing, the scientific part that will blow your wig off… All of this parabolic stuff, the fact that we are simultaneously existing in two realms at once, the physical and the spirit, the fact that there is an intersection of the material realm and the spirit realm, that the unseen realm is as real as the seen realm and that the unseen actually affects the seen realm, *are theories that science has suggested for years.*

Religion has historically explained reality dualistically, meaning it has separated spiritual and physical reality, and never the two shall meet. This dichotomy has had many names 'the spirit and the flesh,' 'heaven and earth,' and my least favorite: 'the church and the world.' That just smacks of judgment, doesn't it?

This absolute partitioning of matter and spirit created a sort of enmity between science and religion. Well, more than a 'sort of' enmity, let's face it, science and religion, they ain't talkin'. This may have been wisdom on the part of science, since religion is known for producing mindsets stuck in the dark ages.

> *"The Bible was written to show us how to go to heaven,*
> *not how the heavens go."*
> - Cardinal Baronius (1598), a quote cited by Galileo.

I guess this guy Baronius meant to tell religion to mind its own business and just get sinners going to heaven, and the scientists would deal with reality. This is the same attitude that confines children to church basements, playing with Popsicle sticks while adults worship. It says, "There, there, little lambs, don't trouble yourselves with the big ideas, you stick to your stories and fables." Intellectual arrogance.

I propose another theory: who better than God's sons and daughters to explore His divine mind?

*"Let a man so account of us, as of the ministers of Christ, and **stewards of the mysteries of God.**"*
1 Corinthians 4:1

*"Many, O LORD my God, [are] thy wonderful works [which] thou hast done, and **thy thoughts** [which are] to us-ward: they cannot be reckoned up in order unto thee: [if] I would de-clare and speak [of them], they are more than can be numbered."*
Psalm 40:5

*"How precious also are **thy thoughts** unto me, O God! how great is the sum of them! [If] I should count them, they are more in number than the sand: when I awake, **I am still with thee.**"*
Psalm 139:17-18

The scriptures tell us that He delights to tell us His secrets and mysteries. Paul told the Corinthians that we are to be the stewards of the mysteries of God. That is particularly awesome! We are to be superintendents of the mysteries of Creation. We need to get busy and start helping these scientists. We have what they need. Revelation! He shares His thoughts with us by way of *revelation*. We take this revelation into ourselves through faith. Then He is faithful to bring us into *experience* which frames His revelation in time and space; experience is, after all, what most people consider to be reality.

"For who hath known the mind of the Lord, that he may instruct him? But we have the mind of Christ."
1 Corinthians 2:16

What does this mean: 'I have the mind of Christ?' I believe that Paul was saying that we are *Christ-conscious,* that He is a part of our very awareness, and since we are one with Him and we are *in Christ Jesus,* we have a standing invitation to ask for instruction, enlightenment and revelation. We are participants in the *mind of Christ.* You have not because you ask not.

Therefore, who should know more about the cosmos and the nature of reality than Christians? We should join these scientists and offer them our services. We could say, "Hey, we see that you are struggling to come up with a theory for the creation of the universe that hangs together with quantum theory. Let's all pray together and ask God for understanding!" Now that sounds like fun. Do you suppose that it will work? Absolutely.

*"And they said unto him, **Ask** counsel, we pray thee, of God, that we may know whether our way which we go shall be prosperous."*
Judges 18:5

*"**Ask**, and it shall be given you; seek, and ye shall find; knock, and it shall be opened unto you:"*
Matthew 7:7

"[It is] the glory of God to conceal a thing: but the honour of kings [is] to search out a matter."
Proverbs 25:2

We need to all come together and start asking the Master Architect for the blueprints and the answers. He will be delighted! For the Father, it's not about the information; it's about His children coming into His Presence. "Abba! Tell us the story of creation! Tell us all about the quarks and string theory and stuff." He will smile and invite us up onto His lap and begin to expound upon His omniscience and the beautiful elegance of His design. This is a project we must seriously consider.

Is the imperative here that we must learn all of the scientific fact that there is to know? Nah! I believe that God desires an opportunity to reveal Himself and His perfect love to a bunch of scientists.

What is Science Anyway?

Merriam Webster defines *science* as the state of knowing. So, we are all capable of science. Maybe that means we are all in some small way *scientists*. I feel smarter already.

Let's start with God. He is *omniscient*. That means that at all times in all places, He has awareness and knowledge of everything. He is THE SCIENTIST. The 'scient' piece of the word denotes that which we have knowledge and awareness of. For too long we have believed that we are only *sentient* or aware of ourselves and our physical surroundings. I call this being 'earth-bound.' What has been devastating is that we have applied this same illogical, religious thinking to our experience of God. Religion has told us how to know *about God*. Religion created a *science* for knowing about God and calls it *theology*, the study of God.

If that is not bad enough, these religious types have had the arrogance to tell you and me that anything we perceive and experience outside of their little 'ology' is not allowed and not of God.

Here's my personal testimonial of religious oppression: I cannot count how many times really well-meaning people have said to me, "You take all of this stuff way too literally." That is one entirely ignorant comment, considering that the word *literally* means 'as it is written." I have a more sure word of prophecy, and if it's written in there, I BELIEVE IT. My Bible is an earthly opportunity to hold the literal hand of Christ. He is the Word made flesh. I have been given the treasury of heaven, that which the Father holds most dear. Yeah, I take it literally.

In one aspect science is the stuff we have awareness and knowledge of, and we call the pursuit of such knowledge Science. *Consciousness* is how we know such stuff. Consciousness is the quality or state of being aware. For example, to say that you were knocked 'unconscious' means you were out of awareness. Hey, that could be what happened to the church. We got knocked unconscious there for a while. Religion can throw a punch.

Here's what I propose: Since you and I are *in Christ Jesus* and since we have *the mind of Christ,* doesn't it follow that we have consciousness and awareness of the realm of the Spirit and the heavenly places? Of course! Even during His brief days on earth, in material reality, Jesus had an unbroken awareness of Heaven and of the Father. He could see into heaven, hear heaven, taste, smell, and touch heaven. He was in continuous communion with His Father.

> *"Then said Jesus unto them, When ye have lifted up the Son of man, then shall ye know that I am [he], and [that] I do nothing of myself; but as my Father hath taught me, I speak these things."*
> John 8:28

Jesus was telling His disciples that there was **no separation** between Himself and the Father in heaven. He explained to them that He did nothing independent of the Father. The only words He said were those He heard the Father saying. In fact, the original language reflects that Jesus literally repeated His Father word for word.

It follows that since Jesus had a perfect, unbroken communion with heaven, He was *heaven-conscious.* Of course since the Son is One with the Father theirs is a face- to- face

communion and dialog of a divine nature. Only He that is
Holy can look upon the very face of God. Still Jesus has taken
our fallen minds and redeemed them and elevated them to
include participation in the very *mind of Christ*. Through His
blood we have relationship, and that includes the privilege of
inquiring into His thoughts. He has made us *heaven-conscious*
as well.

Paul recounts his experience of being intensely conscious
of heaven:

> *"I knew a man in Christ above fourteen years ago,*
> *(whether in the body, I cannot tell; or whether out of the*
> *body, I cannot tell: God knoweth;) such an one caught*
> *up to the third heaven.*
> *And I knew such a man, (whether in the body,*
> *or out of the body, I cannot tell: God knoweth;)*
> *How that he was caught up into paradise,*
> *and heard unspeakable words,*
> *which it is not lawful for a man to utter."*
> 2 Corinthians 12:2-4

I have always loved that Paul referred to himself in the
third person here. It is just funny to me. Perhaps he was trying to maintain plausible deniability, no, that's just Paul being
humble. Anyway, he tells of an experience he had that was
entirely vivid and authentic, but he could not tell if it was a
physical or a spiritual experience. The best part is that to Paul,
it did not matter if this was a material or spiritual experience,
because one is no less real than the other. Paul existed one
hundred percent in the spirit, and he existed one hundred
percent in his physical body, just as Jesus did. Paul did not
discount the realm of the spirit because he could not see it.
Better yet, he did see it!

So did John the Beloved:

*"After this I looked, and, behold, a door [was] opened
in heaven: and the first voice which I heard [was] as it were
of a trumpet talking with me; which said, Come up hither,
and I will shew thee things which must be hereafter."*

*And immediately I was in the spirit: and, behold,
a throne was set in heaven, and [one] sat on the throne.
And he that sat was to look upon like a jasper and a
sardine stone: and [there was] a rainbow round about
the throne, in sight like unto an emerald.
And round about the throne [were] four and
twenty seats: and upon the seats I saw four and twenty elders
sitting, clothed in white raiment; and they
had on their heads crowns of gold.
And out of the throne proceeded lightnings and
thunderings and voices: and [there were] seven lamps
of fire burning before the throne, which are the seven
Spirits of God."*
Revelation 4: 1-5

*So both Paul and John had what we call translations
nto heaven. So have I. So have you.*
*"And hath raised [us] up together, and made [us] sit together
in heavenly [places] in Christ Jesus:"*
Ephesians 2:6

When the resurrected Christ ascended into heaven He raised all believers together in Him and seated us in heavenly places in Christ Jesus. I have studied Ephesians 2:6 forwards, backwards, inside-out, and upside down. I have looked at the tense of every Greek word in the verse. I have read too many commentaries on the passage. It says what it says.

Let God be true and every man a liar.

You and I have a *Christ-consciousness* as we are *in Christ*. At all times we have that available to us. We have consciousness of Jesus at all times. We also have a *heaven-consciousness,* an awareness of heaven. I am in Christ and therefore always with Christ, so there is actually something wrong with me if I do **not** have awareness of Him. I take this so literally and so seriously that I have warned my friends. I refuse to live my life, not one moment of it, acting as if Jesus is not right here! Me in Him and Him in me. Therefore many times I speak directly to Him, aloud, just as I would speak to you. It is high time we stop the pretense that He is not present. Omnipresent.

"Who shall separate us from the love of Christ? [shall] tribulation,
or distress, or persecution, or famine, or nakedness,
or peril, or sword?"
Romans 8:35

No. None of these physical experiences can separate us from Jesus.

"For I am persuaded, that neither de`ath, nor life, nor
angels, nor principalities, nor powers, nor things
present, nor things to come,
Nor height, nor depth, nor any other creature,
shall be able to separate us from the love of God,
which is in Christ Jesus our Lord."
Romans 8:38-39

No created being, no state of being, no tense of being can separate us from God's love: Jesus the Christ! And Paul says "...nor things present nor things to come..." This means that *time* has no relevance and no affect whatsoever on our unity with Christ and our location in Him.

Speaking of time...It has no effect on God whatsoever. There is a vile misconception that time has been able to put separation between us and Jesus. Presently many of us desire to experience the essence of First Century Christianity. The fault in our logic has been that we must somehow go backward to do so. Why? Has God moved? No. Our hearts have moved.

The upper room Christians had their hearts focused like laser beams on the promise of Jesus to send another and endue them with power. They quit all of their extraneous Christian meetings such as covered dish fellowships and bus trips to Rome. They trained their minds and hearts on Him and what He had promised and found themselves in an atmosphere and a place we know as *one accord in one place.*

> *"And when the day of Pentecost was fully come, they were all with one accord in one place."*
> Acts 2:5

What place was that? The obvious answer is "the upper room," but not entirely. The Greek says that they were all in one mind with one passion. That is the 'one accord' part. Now this is really interesting...the Greek for 'in one place' *autos,* means *himself.* Could it be that the *place* that they were in was *in Christ Jesus?*

I really don't think that room they were in had anything to do with Pentecost. Jesus had given them instructions and their intentions were to follow those directions implicitly.

> *"And, being assembled together with [them], commanded them that they should not depart from Jerusalem, but wait for the promise of the Father, which, [saith he], ye have heard of me."*
> Acts 1:4

They pursued Jesus' promise from the Father with their obedience. They remained in Jerusalem, the Hebrew name for 'the place of double peace'. They were so conscious of and dedicated to their oneness in the Spirit of God, in Christ Jesus, that heaven opened over them and Holy Spirit filled them to overflowing. They had given themselves over to Jesus as their reality completely, body and spirit. Through grace and by faith their hearts came into perfect alignment with the intentionality of God's heart.

This was the portal of entrance for the mighty rushing wind of Holy Spirit, this place of deep, abiding double peace, power, significance, authenticity, obedience, and unity in the person of Jesus Christ.

Human beings just cannot build unity like that, try as we might. The church has attempted to construct unity around so many lesser things. We have rallied around teachings, doctrines, denominations, culture, theologies, personalities, and 'moves of God.' There is ONE THING whereby we are united and unified. Jesus the Christ of Nazareth. He is All- in -All. In Him, we have our lives and we have unity. In this person called Jesus we are all one Spirit and one baptism. We can talk in many tongues and yet we will all be understood.

I truly believe that the 'upper-roomers' were the first fruits of Pentecost because of the *powerful revelation* they had of heaven and of *Jesus as Reality*. So many today cry out for renewal and revival. We ask God to give us something like the second chapter of Acts. I believe He is actually restraining Himself! He intends even better.

I see the heart of God for our generation: He stands on the circle of the earth and He is restraining Himself from pouring out *the latter rain* which is written to be greater than the former. He is waiting for a critical mass of believers to unite in the revelation that His Son Jesus is the Highest Reality, and that we are with Him where He is and He indwells us. He waits for us to stop doing 'churchy' things, and He desires that we assume our true identities: *we are the church, the Body of Christ, the dwelling place of God, His living House.* He waits for us to throw off religion, renew our minds, and allow Him to raise our collective consciousness to its intended level: heaven and the Lord of Glory come to earth to rule and reign.

In this corporate revelation we will stand at the gate of heaven. Signs and wonders will follow. As will the greatest harvest!

CHAPTER SIX

EINSTEIN THE SEER OR HOW DID EVERYTHING BECOME INVISIBLE?

There are profound arguments in scientific circles over the faith or atheism of Albert Einstein. I have read books and articles that go either way, but I believe that any guy as smart as Einstein had to have a profound perception of God.

It is as if Einstein were a 'seer' in the Biblical sense. It is as if he had seen into another realm and dimension. Basically, the stuff that this man figured out changed the world, heck it changed our perception of the universe. He reframed our picture of physical reality. He did so over the period of less than a month in 1905. What inspired him? Better yet, Who inspired him?

While experimenting with electricity and the nature of light, Einstein began to question the scientific status quo. He somehow took a crooked cow path from his planned experiments and ended up proving that space and time are not two separate dimensions, but one unified field that he called "space-time." In his *Theory of Special Relativity*, Einstein demonstrated that time and space are fantastically different from all of preceding scientific theory that went before. Space and time are inseparable and are interwoven like a fabric.

Essentially, Einstein, and all of the work of physics since Einstein, demonstrates that time cannot be affected without space being altered and vice versa. They are related, hence the name *Special Relativity*. He went on from special relativity to proving that not only were time and space related to one another, they *are relating*. That promoted them from being inanimate things and theories to being *entities that are actually doing something*. Now this opened up a huge window for changing reality as we know it.

Space and time had previously only been dimensional constructs that needed to be measured by something else. They are both *unseen things* unless they are viewed *in relation to* something else.

An example of time relativity: without the solar system, the sun and the moon, night and day, how would we measure the dimension time? 'Clocks' is not the answer. To measure time we need a set of axes to determine position and motion. Without these external references, time is *unsee-able*. That is to say we can only perceive the passage of time by *observation*. We perceive it passing in many ways, light changes, our view of the sky changes; we observe life processes like grass growing, and so on. It is the same with space. How do you measure space if not by the *things* that fill it and the measured distances between objects? Space in and of itself is also an *unseen* dimension just as time is.

Einstein went further down his path of revelation and demonstrated that even though space and time are unseen and imperceptible except for in relation to something else, they are not nothings and voids. Even though you cannot reach out and touch a thing called 'space' or a thing called 'time', have you ever doubted their existence? No way! This is the very sandbox that we play in!

Einstein also proved that in tandem with one another, space and time *are dynamic;* right now they are *doing something.* They are subjective, meaning they are acted upon by forces such as the gravitational field and electromagnetism. Another variable is thrown in the mix: the speed with which an observer is moving within the fabric of space-time determines one's experience of space-time! The faster you are going, the slower time is going.

The dynamism of space-time interacting with matter evidenced by other forces such as gravity is Einstein's *Theory of General Relativity.* Einstein demonstrated how space-time is relating to everything else in the universe, or matter. He proved that gravity acting on matter is not so much a *force,* but a result. Gravity happens because space-time is *curved.* What are space and time up to whilst we go about our busy days? Expanding. Here's the really neat thing: space and time are *responding to us.* Are you feeling increased significance?

> *"[It is] he that sitteth upon the circle of the earth, and the inhabitants thereof [are] as grasshoppers; that stretcheth out the heavens as a curtain, and spreadeth them out as a tent to dwell in:"*
> Isaiah 40:22

Isaiah, as well as Moses, David, Daniel, and Ezekiel had the common revelation that the ether we inhabit is a woven construct God created out of space and time. (See Genesis 1:8; Psalm 150:1; Daniel 12:3; Ezekiel 12:1) Space-time was to them a something that could be stretched and spread and pitched as a tent. I like the tent analogy. It demonstrates the dimensionality of the fabric of the universe. What is the significance of this poorly explained science stuff in a book about Jesus as Reality?

Here's the Thing...

To fully experience life in Christ, being one with Him and all other Christians in the Spirit, we must get entirely comfortable with the fact that things that are *unseen* are **more real** than the things we can see with our physical eyes. This is a whopper of a paradigm shift. We just discussed time and space, space-time, and its pretty much a given that most everybody *believes in* space and time. And, even if you do not believe in time and space, you are doing a good job of making a dent in them.

Whether you like it or not, you have been trusting in the unseen realm all of your life. You trust that when you get up tomorrow time and space will be there waiting for you. You have faith in space and time. You believe in them even though in truth you have never *seen* them.

Well then, Just Who Can You Trust?

Without going into a long and inept discussion of quantum physics, we can also all pretty much agree that there is another unseen realm which is the home of the smallest particles in the universe. Once these smallest things were thought to be atoms that were made up of protons, neutrons, and electrons. These were believed to be the smallest particles that make up matter—the hard stuff. The stuff we think is so real.

Traditionally all of the *micro* stuff was believed to be matter, it was just far too small for us to see. So, atoms and molecules were matter, just little itty- bitty matter. Since atoms were just mini units of material, Einstein postulated that there must be a theory that would also explain the physics of atoms and the physics of the macro universe, the earth and planets and stars, all at once. He spent the balance of his life in pursuit of a unifying theory and its mathematical expression. It was his elusive *Theory of Everything*.

Fast-forward to the present. Due to relentless pursuit of a *Theory of Everything*, cosmologists and quantum theorists somehow met in the middle and agreed to push every edge of the envelope of $E=mc2$. It worked! As mathematicians pressed Einstein's equation to expand it into more *dimensions*, it blossomed into a thing of divine beauty. Pushed past the limits of the last known dimension, $E=mc2$ accounts for the cosmos and the quantum field.

I believe that Albert Einstein was, and continues to be a revelatory gift to humanity. As far as science and math go—to *String Theory* and beyond—there is the brilliance, beauty and revelation of Albert Einstein.

It's Immaterial

Current quantum theories that are fully supported by mathematical proof say that atoms are *not* the smallest measurable units of stuff. Since around 1930 science has walked in revelation of the *sub-atomic realm*. New units such as the photon and the quark have made atoms look immense. These new quantum entities are not stuff at all. They are merely *potentialities* and *probabilities*. They are merely *mathematical maybe's*.

A photon, which is the Greek word for light, is the basic stuff that makes up the electromagnetic field. Simultaneously photons are 'points' like a dot on a paper, and 'waves' like a squiggly line or a string. This is called *particle wave duality*. One thing, a photon for example, can be a one-dimensional point, while at the very same time it is a two-dimensional wave. As a point, like a dot on a paper, the photon is only in one dimension. As a wave, like a line on a piece of paper, the photon exists in two dimensions. This is what I like to call the *proof of the possibility of being in two places at once.*

The universe is not a fixed, hard and concrete thing; it is a *probability*. The way that sub-atomic particles appear depends upon the perspective from which they are observed and the speed of their vibration. We are linear in our mindsets and accustomed to seeing things as one way or another. However, God is vast and manifold. He created the universe and all of the stuff in it to be plastic and changeable and full of limitless possibility and potentiality.

This could be where man's dominion comes into play. The universe macro, micro and sub-atomic was created for our influence, interaction and input. You and I affect the cosmos on countless levels and in multiple dimensions! "Who is man that You are mindful of him?"

CHAPTER SEVEN

A GUIDE FOR WALKING OFF THE MAP

I f it is on the map it is no longer our destination. I believe this with my whole heart. We are called to move about in Jesus Christ as Reality from one level of His glory to a higher level of His glory. Jesus' glory is so vast that it is called unsearchable. So, what good is a two-dimensional map to the people of God who are called to be *in Him* and *with Him where He is*? We are called to a path of life that is **transcendent** every step of the way. Where are we? *In Christ Jesus.* Where is that? *Where He is.* He is not bound by any linear map or timeline. We have to turn away from the unholy practice of expecting God to travel our route in our timeframe.

It seems so redundant to say this, but we cannot be led by anything or anyone other than the Spirit of God. If we continue to follow tradition—even religious tradition, we will always wind up in the same place. That by very definition is *un-transcendent.* That is not 'from glory to glory.' I think we do things like that for emotional comfort. *We go back to things.* We may believe that we return to the old and familiar to honor and memorialize. Honoring and memorializing are good, but if we're honest with ourselves, we like how we feel when we go back.

Consider the absurdity of this statement:

"I am getting a warm and fuzzy feeling about the good old days. I feel comfortable here. God must be initiating a new move."

No way. When God begins to do a new thing there is stirring and shaking. We are sensitive to that and we begin to align ourselves with Him so that we can move in sync when He begins to move. Looking around in these times, you see a multitude of reactions. Some get joyfully expectant and focus in on Him so they don't miss a thing! Some get anxious and nervous and do all that they can do to rally the troops because this thing is imminent and it involves *change.* "Change bad, change mess up plans. Fight change. Assert authority. Reassert roles. Call a board meeting. This is new and different and therefore not of God." Maintain the status quo even if it is dying and on life support. We'll prop the old thing up and make it look alive if we have to! "Weekend at Bernie's." Enough said.

Reunions and remembrances are good, but this is not how God initiates and implements a new thing or a new move of His Spirit to make strides for His Kingdom in the earth realm. He is the Creator and it is His nature to be creative. He is the Father and He is eternally fertilizing willing and yielded wombs to bring forth new life. He is the Lord of the Harvest and He is Fruitfulness.

As a corporate body of believers we honor all of the men and women who sacrificed all to participate with God one hundred years ago in the revival called Azusa Street. We give all honor and glory to the Lord for His move that went around the world, expanding the Kingdom and our revelation. So, we go back to give thanks and to honor and memorialize. We look for God's eternal virtues in that place and time and we claim them as inheritance, releasing them into the present by way of our thanksgiving, testimonies of praise, and prophetic decrees of our expectations of Him to exceed Himself in the present and future. Then, we are responsible to carry His intentions into the future. We do not however replicate that former move of God as if it is a template or formula. There is no faith in that, or if there is it is very misplaced faith because it makes people dependent upon the construct of their intellectual understanding of a prescribed protocol. That makes *what happened* and *the way or order in which it happened* the focus and the determining factor. Jesus must be our eternal focus. Only as it is in heaven, the very will of the Father will determine the expression of Jesus in the earth. Only He is worthy of our faith and once we properly invest it He will do a new thing. He will bless us with our participation in what He is doing.

"But we all, with open face beholding as in a glass the glory of the Lord, are changed into the same image from glory to glory, [even] as by the Spirit of the Lord."
2 Corinthians 3:18

Paul writes that we are all continuously *in process.* None of us has arrived or apprehended, we should all be *submitted to the process of being transfigured into the image of Christ.* So, if you are out there 'trying to find yourself' cut yourself a break and quit now. Find Him, then, who you are *in Him.* I am sharing a short cut that I confess to not taking.

How are we transformed? Well, we are transformed by the agency of Holy Spirit. Because we are all One in Spirit and One in Baptism our participation in the Spirit and with Him on a personal level is the power of God at work in us, in great grace, transfiguring us. Holy Spirit guides and instructs us in the process of having our physical and personality manifestations properly align with our new spiritual DNA. The desired result is that we look and behave like Him and that we have hearts like Him.

My personal plea for process: *DO IT!*

Embrace process, it never goes away, learn to love process. *Intimacy is birthed in process.* I dare to say that one cannot claim any degree of intimacy with God outside the experience of process. There are times when process takes us into the wilderness, love the wilderness! This is your time of 'honeymooning' with Jesus. OK, I am not afraid to say it: Processing with Jesus in the wilderness is a time of learning what He likes in intimacy. It is also ministry training for the next season.

He will take you far from the madding crowd, out into the wilderness. Maybe this looks like a job change, a new ministry position, the end of something familiar, or even a hiatus between assignments. It may come as gracefully as appearing to be the next step in a progression. It may come in the guise of a huge personal failure or a rejection. None of that matters. What matters is that you are going away with the Lord! Do not miss that. Do not cut that short or circumnavigate this experience as it is a treasure.

Again I fearlessly make the analogy that the wilderness time is getting intimate with God: Jesus, The Father, and Holy Spirit. Jesus, your bridegroom will have His hands all over you! He will not keep His hands off of you! There is healing in that touch. There is impartation in that touch! Those hands raise the dead with a touch. Seas calm with a wave of those hands. Provision multiplies in those hands! He will draw you to His side and He will say passionate, loving, intimate things to you that will penetrate the depths of your heart and spirit. His spoken love-making will provoke powerful responses in your emotions, your very flesh will quiver! Your times in the wilderness alone with Him will leave you spent and pleasantly exhausted.

*"Who [is] this that cometh up from the wilderness,
leaning upon her beloved?"*
Song of Solomon 8:5a

*"Now there was leaning on Jesus' bosom one of his disciples,
whom Jesus loved."*
John 3:23

I love the picture of the lovers in Songs. I think you and I both know what was going on in the wilderness. I love the love of John the Beloved and Jesus. Why was John chosen as the Revelator? My guess is that it is because his head, the part of his body symbolic of perception, consciousness, and awareness, is on the *heart of Jesus*. John the Revelator heard the heartbeat of God with both his physical and spiritual ears.

When I was a small girl, my very favorite place on earth was sitting beside my father with my ear on his heart. On lovely days we would go and sit beside a stream, under a willow tree. I would rest my little ear on his heart. At once I could feel and hear his heart, I could hear the babble of the stream and I could hear the breeze in the willow tree. It was hearing heaven and earth together! I could listen to the thud, thud, thud of his heart all day and not tire of it. I could feel his breath on my other cheek as we sat so still together. I have always been in love with Daddy. I thank The Father for this. It made His heart a loving and familiar place for me. There have been times in the wilderness that I called out, "Abba, Father, hold me!" I have never had a date with my Father that he did not keep.

Works Fight the Wilderness. My plea for ceasing from works:

If you are like I was, you are 'working on' yourself. Have mercy. Surrender. Take your hands off the wheel. Burn your self-help books, including the 'Christian' ones. Stop attending meetings focused on '40 steps to this or that.' Give up any *purpose* that is based on works. Holy Spirit is perfect, He is perfectly capable, He is doing a Kingdom work in you, and Jesus will take one hundred percent responsibility for the outcome.

> *"Looking unto Jesus the **author and finisher** of [our] faith; who for the joy that was set before him endured the cross, despising the shame, **and** is set down at the right hand of the throne of God."*
> Hebrews 12:2

One particular day, years ago, I set about to spend the day in prayer and intercession, for me! I had acknowledged to God that I was a mess and I planned to spend the day taking out my own garbage. I was going to get into a better, *a more right* relationship with Him. I was merciless with myself. I repented of everything I could recall and even what I could not recall. I systematically dismantled me. Even good personality traits were scourged away. If this was a house I was remodeling, you could say that I 'gutted the place.' About five hours into this the Lord intervened on my behalf.

"May I take the whip from your hands?" He asked me in a calm tone.

"What, Lord?" I sobbed.

"What kind of religious self-mutilation are you practicing now?" He challenged.

"I want nothing between You and me, Lord! So I am repenting and confessing everything!" I explained.

"Well, it's pathetic—Stop it!" He demanded.

"Lord, I repent for being pathetic, please forgive me!"

Yes, I am blonde.

He is the most patient friend! He just stood by me as I knelt on the floor and He waited in perfect peace for me to get a clue. Much time passed. I was unhinged.

Finally Jesus cut me a break. He knelt down beside me and said,

"Kelly, I promise to take one hundred percent responsibility for our relationship! You need to rest in Me and trust in Me! I Am the author and finisher of you, your faith, the call on your life, I Am!"

I could hear Holy Spirit singing Second Corinthians 3:18 into my spirit. That was a moment of epiphany. Ironically, now I really needed to repent. I repented of a religious spirit. I repented of dead works, dead words, dead letters, and religion. And, this repentance pleased Him. I have completely taken Him up on His offer to be the responsible party in our relationship and I have had such sweet rest.

We must stop all works and efforts to make things happen with the arm of the flesh. In plain English, we are not called to affect the physical realm, including our churches, ministries, evangelism by any physical means. This includes will power aka *stubbornness*, the power of personality and persuasion aka *manipulation*, wielding authority not to birth something for the Kingdom but to get our own desired outcome aka *control*.

Why are so many in ministry exhausted and burned out? Because whatever you build with the arm of the flesh you must *maintain* with the arm of the flesh. Whatever is built or implemented by weak man-made instrumentality becomes our junk to *maintain*. Does anyone go into ministry thinking, "Gee, I'd really like to be a maintenance worker?"

Every aspect of my life improved because I had handed over the reigns of relationship to the Lord. He had always cared for me, I had just made Him work so much harder at it by blockading things with my crazy plans and strategies and those religious notions. I had come into a place of trusting Him and really believing Him.

*"For the which cause I also suffer these things: nevertheless I am not ashamed: for I know whom I have **believed**, and am persuaded that he is able to keep that which I have committed unto him against that day."*
2 Timothy 1:12

I committed the entire kit and caboodle to Him that day and I haven't looked back.

*"For he that is entered into his **rest**, he also hath ceased from his own works, as God [did] from his.
Let us labour therefore to enter into that **rest**, lest any man fall after the same example of unbelief."*
Hebrews 4:10-11

*"Let us therefore fear, lest, a promise being left [us] of entering into his **rest**, any of you should seem to come short of it."*
Hebrews 4:1

When Jesus is our Reality, **rest** becomes our ongoing experience.

When needed, he will draw us into the wilderness to train in complete dependence on Him and to develop intimacy. The wilderness is 'off the map' in terms of being uncharted territory for you and I. God always knows the way.

The Forerunner Frontier of Faith

The Forerunner Frontier of Faith is another 'off the map' realm. It is that place that is out ahead of the cutting edge, the place that has not only pushed the edges of the envelope, it has caused a blow-out of the envelope. It is 'out there.' It is the lost horizon and it is territory in Jesus and in the Spirit realm that is presently unoccupied. But, stay in rest and peace, it is still 'in Christ Jesus' and therefore it is Reality.

It is in this vast, beautiful, and exciting realm in Jesus that you will see Abram walking and talking with God:

> *"Now the LORD had said unto Abram, Get thee out of thy country, and from thy kindred, and from thy father's house, unto a land that I will shew thee:"*
> Genesis 12:1

Do you think that Abraham was a frontiersman and a forerunner? He is the first fruits example of such an explorer. Do you suppose that Abraham experienced an entirely new reality such as we are called to? In Genesis 12 God calls Abraham out of all that is familiar to him. God walks Abraham completely off his map. In fact, when God said 'get thee out' the Hebrew word He used was a very forceful directive. It meant: go, walk out, proceed, or *die to a certain manner of life!* Yes, Abraham left all familiar terrain and experience and went 'out there.' In fact, God called him to a land that He would show him.

"God, where is this place? What is it like?"

"I will show you."

Abraham was required to leave his grid and his map, his kindred and the protection of his father's house and walk to 'a land.' Abraham was on a need- to- know basis. The Hebrew word for land used in Genesis 12:1 means *world, way, and wilderness.* God was taking Abraham to another world. His reality most certainly changed.

Abraham obeyed God. His faith opened the door to an entirely new realm of existence. Everything was unknown and unfamiliar and he was entirely dependent upon God. These are highly favorable conditions. In this new realm and frontier of faith *God appeared*. When God appeared He promised Abraham that this land would be bestowed upon his seed. The frontier of faith is the land of inheritance. Sojourning with God in faith and 'in Christ Jesus' will always bring us into His Presence, the Promised Land, and our Godly inheritance, as well as into greater intimacy with Him and greater dimensions of His glory.

Revelation and prophecy also open the door to new realms in Him. Saying yes to God in faith will release you into a frontier and forerunner realm of reality and experience. A young girl with her heart focused on God received a prophetic word from an angel one night. She said, "Be it unto me according to Your word, Lord." She said yes, and God the Holy Spirit visited her. Eternally Mary remains the single occupant of a realm in God called The Virgin Birth. Her 'yes' to having a total change of reality opened eternity to you and me.

Those Who Cling to the Map

As people whose reality is 'in Christ Jesus' we are called to live by faith. We are also called to co-labor with Jesus in establishing His Kingdom in the earth. This is a labor of love because we do this not for ourselves but for Him. We must desire to see Him receive all of the rewards of His suffering. Without exception, those called to live as disciples of Jesus Christ are called to leave familiar things, family, occupation, people's approval, country, religion. We are called to a life of 'off the map' journeys. This is a place in Him where you really must trust in the unseen. If you choose to stay in a place where everything is known to you, no faith is required. Without faith it is impossible to please God.

"Off the map" is the multi-dimensional place in Christ that is unrecognizable to you by way of self-referral and personal past experience. It is a place that has transcended history and tradition and human conceptualizations. You are off the grid and in uncharted terrain, but you are not alone. Fun times are when you cannot even see the map from your new vantage point in Him.

There is a difference between 'new places' and the *frontier realm of faith* that is life in Jesus as Reality. Simply going to a new place does not necessarily require the operation of faith. We can't just decide for ourselves to move from point A on the map to point B on the map and call it the wilderness or uncharted territory. Why? Because in this instance you yourself are the cartographer. Since you drew the map you are in control of the information and the outcome. There is no need for faith. This is another instance of making plans for God, or asking Him to bless our plan and program. This is not forerunning, it is wandering.

We are required to follow Him and forget the roadmap. A roadmap is a historical document. If someone had not been there in the past the crazy map would not exist. The frontier realm is for forerunners who will be led by Jesus and Holy Spirit alone. We must fix our eyes on God alone, not looking back or referring back to how it was done in the good old days.

Still, there are some who are experiencing a frustrating tension between desiring to enter into fresh levels of glory and revelation and clinging to a familiar point on the map. This can produce double-mindedness and instability. This scenario creates a **false realm** in which it wrongly appears that God is not answering the cries of His people! In this case prayers are not answered because the people ask amiss.

> "Ye ask, and receive not, because ye ask amiss, that ye
> may consume [it] upon your lusts."
> James 4:3

I ask for grace because this perhaps seems like a hard word. Understand that in the true Kingdom of God His people live abundant lives. In the Reality of the Kingdom He withholds no good thing from any of us. However, the overriding Truth of the Kingdom is that Jesus is in dominion. He gets control and He holds the future. In other words, He is the Way, the Truth, and the Life.

We have no right to tether God to our roadmap or our plan and program. He is sovereign, He leads, we follow. He is the cloud by day and the pillar of fire by night. And His name is Beautiful!

CHAPTER EIGHT

OH NO, THE PARABOLA IS BACK!

H ere's where our parabola serves us well. It can be our tool to visualize the revelation of *Christ as Reality*, and where we presently live. Draw two intersecting circles, one above the other. The lower circle represents the physical earth. All of nature is here and this is where we pay taxes. The higher of the two circles represents Christ and His Kingdom and the heavenly realm. *The subset where the circles intersect is the land of our lives at this present time.*

This is the land of "being in two places at once". You are simultaneously in the physical earth realm and in the metaphysical Body of Christ. You have consciousness of earth with all of its physical laws such as gravity, time, and distance. You also have awareness and consciousness of *being in Christ Jesus* and *being seated with Christ Jesus in Heavenly Places.*

This is the tension that we feel. Religion has fossilized a false paradigm into our collective consciousness. Religion tells us that we are 'saints' we are 'new creatures' and that the 'old man' has passed away. Yet, religion would have us all living in a paradigm in which you and I are *supernatural and eternal beings* trapped in the physical realm just hanging on in survival mode until Jesus comes to get us. Man, I hate that. Religion has indoctrinated us to believe that *the natural* exerts power and dominion over the *supernatural.* Oh, cut me a break. How long are we, the Body of Christ, going to buy into this?

You are a *supernatural being* who is simultaneously alive in the physical and the spirit realms. You were given dominion and power over the physical planet. Your ancestors named all of the creatures and stuff here and in doing so endued all of them with certain characteristics and qualities. From the beginning we were co-laborers with Christ. Admittedly we live according to all of the physical laws of the planet. Sometime I may give you my personal testimony of the progressive power of gravity.

Anyway, we also have the all-powerful fulfillment of the Law of God working in us and through us to affect the earth realm and change it into the Kingdom of Jesus Christ.

All of God's principles and laws are designed on our behalf. We have all of His Inerrant Word at work in this realm *accomplishing that which it was sent to do!* We have all of the gifts and promises of God available to us at all times. We have *Christ as our Reality,* we have the all-powerful Holy Spirit alive in each of us, the same Spirit that raised Jesus from the dead **lives** in you and me.

Can we really go on living in agreement with this lie of religion that says we are prisoners of physicality rather than *the dominant force on the planet?* We must stop being the willing victims of a mass identity crisis.

*For the earnest expectation of the creation eagerly
waits for the revealing of the sons of God.*
Romans 8:19

We are the sons of God now, and now is the day that we rise up and throw off the false reality of religion and see ourselves as who we really are. The Word says that all of creation is yearning for us to get the revelation of who we are and to *become who we really are.* We are the children of the omnipotent supernatural Creator of the universe and we are made like Him. We are the seed of Abraham. We are a dominating force for the goodness of God on this planet. We are the Beloved of the Christ. We are more than over comers. You and I are what preserves and lights the earth realm. We are the Body of Jesus Christ and we are the carriers of the Holy Spirit. We are conduits of the Perfect Love of the Father. No wonder everything that has been created is waiting for us to show up.

What the earth and its creatures crave, you and I have. Will we wake up to this fact and assume our rightful identity or will we roll over and sleep several more generations? God forbid. To fully manifest as the Sons of God we are going to have to fully embrace our *supernatural nature.* We must reverse our backward thinking and walk in the revelation that the *unseen realm* of the Spirit is the preeminent realm and that we *exist in that realm.* We must live out of our supernatural selves first and participate in the physical realm as a secondary reality. How to do this?

Make a decision. Remember the day you decided for Christ and salvation? Have you ever doubted that decision and the change that resulted? You can trust your supernatural, loving, God to keep you as His supernatural child. He will never leave you or forsake you. He has told you that He looks upon your heart and spirit first. Have a heart to heart with Him today and tell Him you want to live out of your spirit and you want to give your spirit preeminence over your physicality. You will cause Him great joy!

We are called to worship Him in Spirit and in Truth. This is the realm of His Spirit and His Son where we are with Him. In this place, He inhabits the praises of His people and we are welcomed into a greater manifestation of His Presence. Some of us had the experience of worshipping and feeling that we 'went somewhere else.' I believe that is because we are somewhere else all of the time, it just takes the intense focus of worship for us to find ourselves there. What would it be like to live in the constant state of being aware of His Presence? It would be life and more abundant. It is life in *Christ as Reality!*

Real, Meaningful Dominion

Are you aware that you were created to impact and affect the entire earth realm?

"And God blessed them, and God said unto them, Be fruitful, and multiply, and replenish the earth, and subdue it: and have dominion over the fish of the sea, and over the fowl of the air, and over every living thing that moveth upon the earth".
Genesis 1:28

One of the ways that God blessed us is by giving us dominion. The intended results of man ruling in the earth realm are fruitfulness, abundance, reproduction, replenishment, and influencing all manner of life. The intended purpose if this is the establishment of the Kingdom of Jesus Christ. You and I are created to influence the earth. We are influential.

It is apparent that religion has taken many captive to the unholy notion that we are ruled over by situations and circumstances, though there is no arguing with a large scale natural disaster. In this case we become the unwitting victims of a large scale event. Sadly, however, many Christians live in a belief system that has them ruled by the smallest occurrence or situation. You and I both know folks who are 'under it' or 'experiencing warfare' most of the time. To them, this can mean anything from a flat tire to a bad hair day. Typically this perceived oppression is attributed to the enemy. Who has dominion here?

I believe God's intended dominion is that we are the most aware and important beings on the planet. We are the divinely appointed influencers, and everything else responds to us. It is not only the fall of man that has put us in the position of being acted upon. It is our own failure to carry the mantle of the dominant ones. We have abdicated our appointed office. When we fail to occupy, a vacuum is created. Is anyone at the helm? Yes. There was one waiting in the wings to fill the void, one who desired such preeminence. Perhaps the enemy is in control over so many things not only because he is so evil, but because we have been sleeping or negligent.

We must shake off the anesthesia of religion and be re-born to The Reality of Life in Christ. This reality entails His people ruling, reigning, and exercising dominion. When we speak, the earth realm listens. Such speech we call prayer. When we speak words that are aligned with heaven and with the heart of God, Holy Spirit administrates and organizes the universe accordingly.

We do not pray and decree our own desires, but rather that *"it be on earth as it is in heaven."* We are to establish His words, His will, and His Kingdom. We had better get busy.

Two Things~ Intentionality and Non-Locality

Quantum Physics demonstrates our dominion.

One recent advance in quantum theory established that there is no such thing as a *local realism* or local reality. Math and physics have proven that *here* and *there* may be separated by space, but that does not mean that they have no relation or relativity to one another. Formerly, Newtonian physics posited that for *here* to affect *there* something had to travel the distance between the two places, something like a messenger particle. That was back when the world was flat.

In the 1980's quantum theorists proved that two seemingly unrelated and unconnected particles separated by a significant distance do in fact affect each other.

"This plainly speaking is weird," author and physicist Brian Greene said in his "The Fabric of the Cosmos." (p12) This demonstrates that space or distance between objects and particles does not insulate, isolate, or even separate.

Greene goes on to say, "With the ensuing twists in scientific progress, Einstein's paper can now be viewed among the first to point out that quantum mechanics—if taken at face value—implies that something that you do over here can be *instantaneously* linked to something happening over there, regardless of distance." (p11)

This is eerily familiar to the phrase made famous by Oral Roberts: "There is no distance in prayer." This was, perhaps, more revelatory than Roberts realized. I believe what he meant was that there is no separation between us and heaven because the perceived gap is bridged by Jesus. This statement also implies that you can be *there* and I can be *here,* and *in Christ* and in the physical—nothing separates us.

Could it be that what we perceive as the distance and empty space that seemingly separate us from each other and from heaven is not empty at all, but is filled with another substance called the spiritual realm?

> *"And hath put all [things] under his feet, and gave him*
> *[to be] the head over all [things] to the church,*
> *Which is his body, the fullness of him that fills all in all."*
> Ephesians 1:22-23

It is Jesus who fills all. The spiritual reality of this is far beyond my comprehension. Jesus fills heaven and earth as His Spirit fills His people, essentially making us all one entity. We comprise His mystical body. The Greek *pleroo* means to fill and to consummate. It also means to render perfect and to cause to abound.

Speaking to the Ephesians, Paul reveals that Jesus fills all things. His words framed the universe and He is the substance of that universe.

Jesus fulfills all of The Father's physical and natural laws. Simply, He makes it all work. This has brought me to a place in which it is impossible for me to live in a reality that is not designed by and sustained by Jesus Christ. Even nothingness requires His existence to establish its definition.

I share all of this quantum stuff in my limited way to say this: It is Jesus Christ Who fills all. I believe that he created all, down to the atom and the quark and the photon. It is He who sustains the universe. What maintains the space between the planets? Even the wind and the waves obey Him.

I look into the night sky from my country home and I see Him. I stare into the eyes of our grandsons and I see the love of God looking back at me. My roses come back vigorously in the spring and declare the beauty of the Lord. I walk into the forest behind my home and the song of the birds takes on an added dimension, and I am in the wilderness with my Beloved. Even as I read and study scientific things that are far above my head, I hear His Spirit reading to me, illuminating my mind and correlating the scientific theories with the scriptures.

I am I Him and therefore always with Him where He is. His Spirit indwells me. I am seated with Jesus Christ in Heavenly places. I walk through the valley of the shadow of death and He has me by the arm. His chest and His heart are my pillow.

*"Such knowledge is too wonderful for me; it is high,
I cannot attain unto it
Whither shall I go from thy spirit? or whither shall I flee
from thy presence? If I ascend up into heaven, thou art there:
if I make my bed in hell, behold, thou art there.
If I take the wings of the morning, and dwell in the uttermost
parts of the sea; Even there shall thy hand lead me,
and thy right hand shall hold me."*
Psalm 139:6-10

Einstein, What Does This All Mean?

Trust in the Unseen

To release yourself fully into Jesus Christ as your Reality and to experience Him as your highest truth and dimension, you must invest faith for both the **revelation** and the **experience** of this. Faith is the current that runs from God through you and into the earth realm. This is the current of power that ultimately affects material reality.

*"Now faith is the substance of things hoped for,
the evidence of things not seen.
For by it the elders obtained a good report.
Through faith we understand that the worlds were framed by
the word of God, so that things which are seen were not made
of things which do appear."*
Hebrews 11:1-3

God framed the world with His spoken word. He made the worlds with unseen stuff. The Greek word for framed means fitted-out, equipped, put in order, or created. *Framed* also demonstrates the dimensionality of God's creation. To construct a home you first put up the basic architecture, giving it height, depth, width, and breadth. You consult a blueprint which is a two-dimensional representation of the home, then you add the materials that make it a three dimensional construct. Now you have a place to enter into.

God spoke the worlds into being. The construct that supports the worlds is His announced intentions, or His 'let there be.'

Could it be that the entire universe is made of, organized by, and held together by an unseen thing? I believe so. The universe is comprised of and sustained by the thoughts, words, and intentions of God—in a Person, Jesus.

I Hebrew there are various words for *word*. Inherent in all of them all are God's *intentions* and *intentionality*. As science, math, and cosmology continue to expand the envelope of our knowledge and awareness, one conclusion unites all others: As we travel further down the rabbit hole in search of answers and understanding, we come upon One Truth. It is that all that we understand and all that we have built upon is non-material and unseen. All matter, when reduced to its most quantum components, is non-material.

What a house of cards we formerly trusted in! As science moves closer to understanding the nature of reality, it reveals the unseen realm—the realm of Spirit.

I love the fact that all of the discovery of the ages has come to this wonderful conclusion that the unseen realm is the real, and that matter and physical experience are derivative of that realm. Things may be coming together here!

"Thy kingdom come. Thy will be done in earth, as it is in heaven."
Matthew 6:10

CHAPTER NINE

IMPACT AWARENESS

We need to build a critical mass of people experiencing *Christ as our Reality.* We need to build a critical mass of people who are *intimate* with the Lord and with heaven. This is the renewing of our individual minds, and releasing corporate religious mindsets. As we allow our minds to be renewed and our consciousnesses raised to *Jesus as Reality*, more of us will find ourselves together in one place and in one accord. We can't just sing a chorus or two, stating that 'we are one' and only have said it. We must have a common revelation and experience. So, individually we must come into *Christ as Reality* and learn to abide in **intimacy.** Then, as we come together in corporate worship and prayer a real unity happens. This is the place where God blesses His people.

> *"Till we all come in the **unity** of the faith, and of **the knowledge of the Son of God**, unto a perfect man, unto the measure of the stature of the fulness of Christ:"*
> Ephesians 4:13

In Ephesians 4 there is a state of *unity* in tandem with the *knowledge* of the Son of God. Paul related the two concepts as they are no doubt interdependent. Paul's apostolic prayer is that we come together in Christ and in our awareness and consciousness of Him. In Thayer's Lexicon 'knowledge' means "a precise and correct knowledge of things ethical and divine." In other words we need to get it together in our comprehension and revelation of things on earth (such as our ethic and custom) and in heaven, the divine. Then, we must keep moving forward from that point into *experience.*

In his book "The Supernatural Power of a Transformed Mind" Bill Johnson says: "The more you and I become empowered and directed by the Spirit of God, the more our lives should defy the natural principles that release spiritual realities." (Johnson 164) He goes on to say that there is a *superior truth* opening to us. I believe that the *experience of Christ as Reality* is part of that truth that supersedes and empowers us to labor under a fresh grace in this end time harvest. The superior anointing needed comes by way of the superior revelation!

So here's what I envision: A groundswell of intimacy initiated by **God**, happening *in Christ Jesus,* administrated, organized and orchestrated by **Holy Spirit** alone. And you know what? This happens one heart and mind and spirit at a time as Holy Spirit speaks to folks. Talk about *grass roots.* Baby this is grass seed. We need a harvest for the Kingdom! No networks, no application fees, no purchased ordination, no titles, no organizational charts.

A Scene in Heaven

Archangel Michael walks up to Gabriel. He says, "Gabriel, please stand guard at the Pearly Gates, we need Peter for a meeting." Gabriel appears flustered and says, "Not in my job description, and why wasn't I invited to the meeting?" Never happen. It's not like that in heaven. The overriding value there is the preeminence of Jesus. He is the Head of all things in heaven and on earth. His interests are the only interests. Thankfully He is very interested in us.

One sign that things are **not** as they are in heaven is that people and groups value titles and roles more than they value God's heart and the hearts of others. I can discern a sort of false reality and false realm build around folks who begin to project themselves from a role or title rather than simply being authentic and honest. Roles and titles can create a false and lesser reality.

Don't Go There, Girlfriend!

I am inserting this note of caution: There are false realms and counterfeit realities! And, many of these masquerade as 'church' or church activities. This is frightening. It is very important that we become aware of the possibility of such counterfeits.

Some of the earmarks of counterfeit realms and realities that the Lord showed me are: constant states of turmoil without resolution, this cannot be in the true Presence of the Prince of Peace. Groups and persons being in constant ongoing states of striving, works, and self-promotion indicate a false realm. A state of abiding rest is inherent *in Christ as Reality!* The subjugation of some ministries and or persons for the promotion of a one-person ministry or empire is another example. You could call this 'empire building.' We have one King, His name is Jesus, and no one else sits on a throne. If someone is claiming apostleship or claiming to be a prophet—check their positioning. You should have to look down to see them. True apostles and prophets, those called to an apostolic or prophetic function will have laid their lives *down* next to Christ, the Chief Cornerstone. They will be building platforms for the ministries of others and they will be producing abundant fruit and spiritual offspring.

Pray to have eyes to see and ears to hear Holy Spirit. Your spirit will bear witness and testify of Him, or He will give you an indication that something is amiss. Ask Him to close all doors to false realms and realities, and don't go there girlfriend!

Those in authority need to be intentionally conscious of their personal authenticity. Be real at all times! We have a Savior Who has been tempted in all ways and has been touched by infirmity—why would we be immune? If I am a visitor in a church hearing the pastor for the first time and he or she uses an illustration of his or her own failing or struggle—I know that they are *for real!* This person is speaking from the heart and without regard to position and status, naked as Adam in the Garden! I admire that! Naked pastors!

God is a God of order. We must do things in His order and within His ordained authority. Having said that, this intimacy and reality shift that must happen is so huge that no one man or group can organize it. We will have to come into a revelation of respecting and reverencing the anointing on *everyone,* not only those with a ministry title. This is a wave that rides on the sovereign wills and ascents individuals. I believe that the wave has been building for thousands of years and soon we will see the swell of the wave. If we devote ourselves to intimacy and consecration and to living in *Christ as Reality*, we will see the effects of the testimony of our lives! If we do as commanded and seek the Kingdom first and Righteousness first and His Will first, we may see the crest of the wave and the breaking of the wave across humanity in our generation.

Possible Wave Inhibitors

Not transcending current religious structures will inhibit this coming move of God. I do not mean that we should demolish or tear down! God is the Shaker! He is shaking everything that can be shaken. We all must avow Psalm 105:15 and don't touch the anointing (which by the way we ALL have) and do not harm any prophets. This is a time to make devout efforts to honor all of the brethren.

However, a religious spirit keeps people boxed up in roles and titles and inhibits them from moving about freely in Him. It blocks up individual vision and puts a ceiling on corporate vision. Without a vision the people perish. I believe that we are currently experiencing a phenomenon in which masses of people have temporarily stepped outside religious structures in order to have their vision either imparted or restored. They are unable to see out around man-made programs and narrowly delineated lines. This is a tough issue. Suffice it to say that if your experience feels confining and restrictive and your growth is stifled; if there is no ongoing flow of revelation and organic growth in an organization. This is a problem. Final word on this: We are the Body of Christ. We are alive. One sure sign of life is *growth*. We are a living *organism*. So do not join yourself to an *organization*. That is a lifeless, man-made thing.

I visited a start- up church, well it was more like a spin-off church. Anyway they had a concept and a slogan that rang my chimes: "It's not about religion—it's about relationship." Bull's eye. That resonates with me. The worship and fellowship were authentic and alive and organically Spirit led. Folks were interested in what was happening because it had all of the evidences of life. Many came to check it out and went around the town reporting that God was doing something in the midst of this little fellowship. They brought their sick and dying loved ones to meetings to receive ministry. Then, one day, even though there were only a dozen or so 'members', an organizational meeting was convened. "Why is there an elephant sitting on my chest?" I said to the Lord.

At this meeting folks were appointed to positions. Titles were given. Structure was implemented. A flow chart was produced. You know those flow charts or organizational charts that are used in corporations, little boxes on a paper, it was like that. Little boxes were constructed for people to sit in. You know what happens when you are made to sit in a little box? You focus on you and the little box! Then, you begin to believe that the little box is the universe. You see everything from the view and perspective of the little box. You become comfortable in the box and may even become protective of that little box. Eventually, you cannot see past the box. *You have been contained by a reality you participated in creating!*

Since it is tough for communication to flow in and around all the little boxes, free exchange of ideas and visions clogs up. People begin speaking out of the lesser reality of roles and titles. People start keeping things to themselves or framing their words in a manner acceptable to the boxes higher up the flow chart. Finally, without a fresh flow of the River of Life and the Spirit, without a vision, the people perish. This breaks God's heart! Religious structures which are not organic plantings of the Lord must be transcended. God says it best: you do not put new wine in old wineskins. So we must be very sensitive to the Lord and the way He is growing a thing. "Build it and He will come," is dangerous and wasteful. A true work or move of God will always be spontaneous, alive, and organic. All of the participants will serve Christ and His Kingdom and not the success of the ministry of one person.

Tradition and **entitlement** are other glory wave inhibitors. Doing things out of role or out of obligation to things and people of the past just invites the living in the past. Do you know what they call people who were alive in the past? *Dead.* Living in the past focuses on the past and not the present and the future. Behold! God is doing a new thing, do you not perceive it? God is Creator. He is therefore by virtue of His

Name creative and always creating new expressions of Himself in order to fulfill His desire to cover the whole earth with His glory. Religion promotes past-oriented thinking and prevents people from receiving revelation from God as to what he is up to in the present.

Entitlement is a mindset that says that you got what you have, position, promotion, and provision— because of who you are or personal accomplishment or giving. It puts the entitled person first in line at all hand-outs and promotions because of their perceived personal merit. That's not God. That's man-made organizational thinking, something like seniority in corporate terms. God is a renowned non-respecter of persons. He says that we should prefer our brethren over ourselves. He says that the first shall be last and the last shall be first. Heaven and *in Christ Jesus* are equal opportunity dimensions! God looks on your heart and if it reflects back to Him His own heart and character, He uses you. If your interests have become His interests you are commissioned by Him.

A few years ago I met a young woman who had breast cancer which was in a rapid metastasis. She was only thirty-eight and she has four children. She worked in a place where I shopped and we began a casual friendship. When she became ill she told me and I asked if we could pray. Our prayers revealed her deep faith and a Christian heritage. I had the opportunity to pray with her several times. Once, I asked if she attended church locally. She said that she did not because the last church she and her husband visited was so unwelcoming. She shared that many friends had recommended that they try a particular church, and in her condition she knew that corporate worship and prayer would minister to her. She also appreciated the need for her family to fit into the local body of Christ.

One Sunday they visited this church and a couple of church members approached them a few minutes before the service. They were not the welcoming committee. They came to the newcomers to explain that they were sitting in their seats! They explained that their family name was on a brass plaque on the end of the pew! My friend and her husband moved to other seats, stayed through the service, and then moved as far away as they could get. Flee! Flee! At first glance you might think these were immature people that were easily offended. These were mature adults who were probably more amused than offended by the whole assigned seating scheme in the church. They had keen enough spiritual discernment to recognize a religious spirit manifesting as entitlement. (After surgery and many believers praying my friend is well!)

Very Dangerous Inhibitor: Negative Impact

Every time you enter a new group you release a wave of impact across that group. This does not even have to be a new experience. For example, every time you attend your regular prayer meeting you impact the group. If we can go back to science for a minute this is the law of physics that says for every action there is a reaction. You cast a stone into a pond and you see the ripples. Action or impact; and reaction or result. These results are either positive or negative, according to our intentions. Every now and then you get someone who reads you or a situation wrong, but typically people will respond to the intentions of your heart.

It is the same with our words. Oh, the power of the words of a child of God!

"Death and life [are] in the power of the tongue: and they that love it shall eat the fruit thereof."
Proverbs 18:21

"…before him whom he [Abraham] believed, [even] God,
*who quickeneth the dead, and **calleth those things***
which be not as though they were."
Romans 4:17b

Remember in the last chapter we discussed the scientific discovery that *here* and *there* are not isolated? Imagine the ripples in the pond. Our words and actions, our attitudes and intentions are *life or death*. They have a profound and even supernatural affect on the earth realm. We either bless or we curse.

Sensitivity to Holy Spirit and the heart of the Father means that we have an awareness and keen sensitivity to the corporate body of Christ. Naturally this includes those yet to believe! If we speak blessing over our own congregation and trash the fellowship down the road can we really go on believing that the good is isolated to us and the negative judgement stays on them? This would be a good working definition of ignorant. Send out death borne on a word and it will return!

"As the bird by wandering, as the swallow by flying, so the curse
causeless shall not come."
Proverbs 26:2

Notice that Solomon uses birds as parabolic symbols in this proverb. They are creatures carried on the air. To fly birds move their wings, beating the air and creating a wave. So it is with our words. We speak and sound waves disperse like ripples on a pond. Our words carry life and blessing or death and cursing according to the intentions of our hearts.

This is also a critical issue if you are led to move from one local church to another. We have to pray: "Lord, show me the impact that my moving will have on the regional church!" More than likely He has told you to make the move, and *how* you walk this is critical. Bless and get blessed. Move and move calmly and quietly. Read Frangipane!

Dependence on Denominations and Isolation Inhibit the Move of God

Last year the Lord told me to stop using the word *denominations*. And, never under any circumstance ask the question, "So, what denomination are you?" (bat eyes, smile sweetly) This was a personal discipline and I am thankful for what I was taught. The Lord told me to refer to denominations as *expressions of Him*. So, I am incorporating that into my awareness and the way I speak.

Lack of Consecration and Not Respecting the Consecration of Others

This coming move of God—God pouring Himself, the Holy Spirit on all flesh—correlates directly to a critical mass of consecration and intimacy. Failure to consecrate to the degree He calls you and in the ways He calls you causes 'hope deferred.' And, since He is our Hope we delay this outpouring and His coming to rule and receive His rewards.

This is my impassioned plea! Consecrate now! Eliminate all non-essential activity, even if it is good and polite and expected. Cut it out! This is more difficult than it sounds and carries more reward than I can convey. In order for us to experience *Christ as Reality* we must forego lesser realities whenever possible. This means we must develop and maintain a focus on Him and what He is saying and doing.

As we develop this focus and establish *Christ as Reality* things that were once normal begin to look like distractions, and really they are. In this parabolic place of being *in Christ*

Jesus, we begin to experience things *as they are in heaven. This is a way in which we **know** what to pray and what He wants decreed and released into the earth realm.*

Politely as possible I say that if they aren't having a bingo tournament and a covered dish social in heaven, we should not be doing it here. (And there are plenty of celebrations going on in heaven!) Is it possible that we waste enormous chunks of time talking *about* building the Kingdom and living in the Kingdom rather than *doing the work of the Kingdom and experiencing a foretaste of the Kingdom?*

For a while it may feel odd and uncomfortable to forego some stuff. We have to develop enough backbone to say no to many regularly scheduled programs and events. People may come up to you and ask if you have been offended or even ask about the state of your salvation. (I wish I was kidding about that!) To some, consecration looks like rejection or isolation. I pray they have grace to get over it.

Living a contemplative life does not mean living a life of ongoing *discussion.* A contemplative life is to focus like a laser beam on the Lord and His desires and purposes and to remove attention and focus from lesser things. He will tell you what these are and He will grace you to come away from these activities that do not yield Kingdom fruit. He will help you to achieve a balance and keep you in His peace and rest and best of all, He will establish His abiding Presence all around you. Then wherever you go that place is the Kingdom of God.

We also must have great grace for one another as we practice consecration and *Christ as Reality.* If you announce to me that you are spending the week in deep consecration I should not call you twice a day and ask, "So, how's it going?"

Well it is blissful, of course! Now buzz off! We need to respect the call of God on everyone's life.

Some friends can become concerned that you are isolating yourself. I guess that's legit. Can I tell you the way to discern consecration from isolation? **Fruit.** The fruit of isolation is – well—there isn't any! The person in isolation is depressed and there is no growth and therefore no spiritual fruit and no fruit for the Kingdom. A person in consecration is growing in the likeness of Christ and there is evidence of the fruit of the Spirit and fruit for the Kingdom.

CHAPTER TEN

"PARITY"

I love the writings of Saint Theresa of Avila. What an intimate life in Christ she has. Jesus calls her His rose. In the
physical realm St. Theresa was so caught up in the Spirit at
times that she levitated as she prayed. She enjoyed frequent
visitations of the Lord and frequent total translations into the
third heaven. Theresa's *reality* was parity with heaven. She
lived *Christ as Reality.* Saint Theresa! I honor you before the
Throne of Grace! I acknowledge that you and I, my dear sister
are in the same place, *in Christ Jesus!* I honor you as a forerunner in *living in the Reality of Christ* and I honor you love for Him
and your intimacy with heaven.

I'll share a story about my hero, The Reverend Bishop
Fulton Sheen. You will either be greatly encouraged by this,
or think I am nuts. I can't see there being any middle ground.
That's fine.

Of course, Fulton Sheen was a Bishop in the Catholic expression. Even before I was born he had a regular TV broad-
cast in which he would teach in front of a chalkboard. I have

been blessed to find some of these shows. This guy had to be the original Charismatic! His personal charisma was off the charts. He was incredibly handsome and cut a fine figure in his vestments and mantle. To date, I have not heard such compelling Bible teaching. He was impeccable and dramatic and his illustrations came alive!

Several years ago I found a first edition copy of his "Life of Christ" in a used book store. I read this work over and over. You see, this book is alive. Reading this book is a supernatural experience, it is reading in several dimensions simultaneously. There are times when I am reading that I can see and hear and personally experience the accounts of the life of the Lord. It is a living letter. I weep over this book so much that I have to be careful not to ruin it.

A few months ago I was on my daily hike in the woods. It was a gorgeous spring day and I could feel a very sweet intimacy with Jesus, and I could sense an invitation pending. I sat on a bench by a stream and the Lord moved His right hand in a sweeping gesture. I could see into the third heaven with great clarity.

I saw a slender, very attractive man sitting on a marble or stone bench. He was in an area like a park or a grove. He wore dark, loose fitting slacks and a button down shirt. A shaft of sunlight came across his face and he leaned his head back to catch the light and warmth of it. A smile of appreciation came on his lips. He was the most satisfied and peaceful person that I had ever seen, other than Jesus.

I could hear birdsong all around me in the earth realm, and I realized that there was a rich birdsong coming from the heavenly realm too. It was spiritually symphonic. These were heavenly harmonics. I looked at the man on the bench and he had tilted his head to listen to the singing of the birds. I asked the Lord the name of the heavenly place that I was seeing.

"This is a bird sanctuary at home," He told me.

My weeping was almost more than my physical being could bear! How can I tell you about the utter beauty that I was experiencing on earth and in heaven? May I tell you something *most beautiful?* Holy Spirit whispered to me like a melody interlaced with the song of the birds:

> *"Are not two sparrows sold for a farthing?*
> *and one of them shall not fall on the ground*
> *without your Father.*
> *But the very hairs of your head are all numbered.*
> *Fear not therefore, ye are of more value than many sparrows.*
> *Are not five sparrows sold for two farthings, and not one of*
> *them is forgotten before God?*
> *But even the very hairs of your head are all numbered.*
> *Fear not therefore: ye are of more*
> *value than many sparrows."*

Even as I recount this experience to you I am transported to a state of being that is more *there* than *here*. Everyone *must* know the intense, intimate, personal, perfect love of God! The *Reality of His Perfect Love* is for everyone! For God **so** loved the world… "So" is such a tiny word to express infinity.

As I looked on I could tell that the man on the bench was also hearing the song of the Spirit and the birds. He was weeping and smiling and he moved his head from side to side as if to express appreciation for this symphony of divine love. He raised his long, slender hands above his head and began to wave them gently back and forth in keeping with the concert of the Spirit and the birds. Then I realized that I had an open invitation to ask about the man.

"Lord, do I know this man?"

"Yes, you do." He said.

"Lord, I don't recognize him in his glorified state."

"This is Bishop Fulton Sheen," the Lord explained.

And I said to Jesus words I say to Him all of the time because He amazes me...

I said, "Lord! *How do you do this?!*"

And, smiling, He replied His standard reply to my frequent question, "I am God—that's how!"

I felt an almost crazy compulsion to request a special favor of the Lord!

"Lord! I want to give him a gift!"

"OK, as you describe to me the gift you want to give, it will manifest." He said.

I sat quietly with the Lord, thinking that He would give me an idea and I would know what to give as a gift. Nothing. He said nothing. After a few minutes I asked, "Lord, what should I give?"

"This is *your* gift—*you* create it!" He replied.

I sat and pondered, still weeping from the intensity of the ongoing experience. I wanted to give the Bishop a copy of " The Life of Christ" with a very special cover. It would be like a memorial copy. I thought that he would like this and that many could view it in the libraries of heaven. So, I explained my idea to the Lord. He really liked it!

"OK, Lord, here's my vision of the book... It is larger than the earth-versions—big like a family Bible or dictionary. The pages are transparent because you do not need words printed of ink because they are Spirit and Life! So, when someone reads

" The Life of Christ", the heavenly version, they read it in the Spirit. As they turn the pages light pours forth and illuminates the reader. The reader is bathed in glorious, heavenly colors and light. As the reader reads of the Holiness of the Lord, he is bathed in blue the color of tanzanite. When reading of new life in Christ the reader is lit up with rays of gold and silver and emerald, and so on.

As the pages of the book are turned, sound and music come out to express the Spirit of the words the Bishop has written. As the pages turn, the reader can smell fragrances of heaven that convey the Spirit of the work and the depth of the love of Christ!"

I sat contemplating more of the design of the gift book. The Lord sat in a peaceful satisfaction, and I was really enjoying the fact that He was watching my words create this gift. He seemed entirely satisfied to be in this place with me. He enjoyed the way in which I was so moved by my own participation in creating something. As I spoke my creative words, I could see what I had described manifest in the realm of heaven.

Finally, I came to the creation of the cover for the book. I wanted this to be one of the most beautiful books in heaven. The design of it needed to convey the very preciousness of the work. It had to reflect the light of Christ onto the heavenly reader. It should embody the Beauty of Christ and reflect that beauty.

I described the book cover, "It is cut lead crystal. The edges of the book are faceted with leaf-like shapes that catch and reflect the light of heaven and the Glory of God. As the cover is opened every color of heaven streams onto the face of the reader! As the cover is opened a trumpet sounds very melodiously and a concert of prophetic voices proclaims: 'Prepare ye the way of the Lord!'

In the very center of the cover is a Cross. This perhaps not original to me because as I spoke that there should be a Cross, the Cross that manifested was similar to the Greek Cross. It was very organic in shape, almost as if it were made of leaves or something from nature. The facets of the Cross were deeply cut and the rays of light that they emitted were fantastic and expressed all of the extraordinary heavenly hues and colors.

I felt that my gift was ready for giving. I saw the book being slipped into a purple velvet drawstring bag and tucked under the wing of a very large angel. That was the last I saw of the book. I sat in the Presence of the Lord and tried to pull myself together. I did not feel an invitation to ask any more about the book. I got up, called for my dog and headed home.

A week later I was out in the woods praying once again. I was praying about writing this book and asking the Lord to cast His eyes over it to be sure that it was His own Testimony and that anything about me or my experience revealed Him. I asked the Lord to cast His eyes over me, and I asked for the grace to have clean hands and a pure heart.

The Lord was very near to me and at the same time He remained silent on the matter of this book. I didn't feel He was withholding approval, I felt like I was waiting to step into the timing of His answer. So we walked along together for over an hour. We came full circle back to where my car was parked and the Lord said, "Let's sit on this bench."

I sat on a park bench with the Lord beside me and my dog hopping all over me. It was getting rather chilly, but I knew the Lord had something on His mind. So, I zipped up my sweatshirt and settled in to wait. A few minutes passed and my best buddy Rags started sniffing at something under the bench. He went under my legs and had me tied up in his leash. I reached down under the bench to untie my feet and a very bright shaft of light flashed in my eyes!

I untangled my feet and got on my knees to look at this bright object under the bench. Do you want to know what I found? I found a piece of crystal about two inches by three inches in size. Even though it had been lying in the dirt it was brilliant. For such a small thing it is very weighty. The crystal rectangle had been cut with a lovely pattern, so I wiped it off with the hem of my sweatshirt so that I could see better.

A border of little facets rims the piece. And, in the center is a Cross similar to a Greek Cross with the members looking organic like leaves. I held the crystal up against the sun, and my entire being was filled with the warm beauty and light of the Lord. I sat holding this miniature of the gift I had given to the Bishop! I was beyond incredulous.

I turned the crystal over and over in my hands to feel the weight and the pattern of it as if to convince my natural mind that it indeed existed.

And I said to the Lord words He loves to hear from me—they amuse Him:

"Lord! How do you do this?"

"I AM God, that's how!" And His broad beautiful face just beams with great satisfaction.

Heaven responds! God responds! Heaven is closer to you than the clothes that you are wearing right now! Heaven is another dimension that you and I and the Lord and the great cloud of witnesses inhabit right now. It is the Preeminent Dimension from which God Almighty determines all things. He determines and decrees that it shall be on earth as it is in heaven.

Since He is in heaven and we are there seated with Him it follows that we are also with Him—or *in Christ Jesus*—in the physical earth realm. Since heaven is the realm of His Glory we should see and experience His Glory in this realm as well. One spring day I made a gift to honor a friend in heaven. Two months later I received a token of that gift back from heaven. Stuff like this happens to us all of the time. Some call this 'miracles' and it very well could be. I believe that the Lord has graced all of us for **parity with heaven.**

Thy kingdom come. Thy will be done in earth, as [it is] in heaven.
Matthew 6:10

Parity is the cry of Jesus' heart. It has to be the focused desire of our hearts in alignment with His. **Parity** is the concept of *equal status* or *functional equivalence*. Can you imagine the Body of Jesus Christ in the earth having *functional equivalence* to 'as it is in heaven'? Well, we had all better start. Are we establishing a Kingdom for the Coming King or are we hanging on till we get rescued?

In physics the term ***parity*** is the name used to denote *symmetry of interactions*. That means that an action *there*—in heaven—has a symmetrical action *here* on earth. Remember we earlier discussed how physics, mathematics, and cosmology have more or less wiped out the former concept of the separateness of *here and there?* This just supports Matthew 6 and the parity that Christ decreed and instructed us to pray for.

In Matthew 6:10 the Greek words 'as it is in' denote sameness, equality, also, even, indeed, when, as it were, both and likewise. These are all analogs of the word parity. We are to be reigning on this earth to grow a Kingdom of parity with heaven for our returning King. We are to be a dominant force for good on the earth to express the nature of our Good King.

How are we to do this? How will we enact and manifest heaven and the Kingdom of God if we know little or nothing about the place? Religion has not provided a blueprint for the Kingdom! Religion has given us dogma and doctrine which are tantamount to a behavioral rule book. Religion has so focused on human behavior—all of the do's and the don'ts that it has succeeded in getting us to believe that this whole religion and Christianity thing is about us.

We were created for God. *We were created for God.* We exist for God. He created us to Love us. This is irrefutable. Nevertheless, observe religious teaching, attitudes and behavior, and you see that we believe that God exists for us.

Consider this: much of what is said in a Wednesday night prayer meeting is human-focused. "Lord, please bless this. Father, please provide that. Jesus, please heal so and so." All of this is good and necessary yet it is not primary and it is not all there is. Religion has us focused on ourselves.

We have become our own idols. A spirit of religion has stolen the focus and made us believe that we are to be the object of that focus. A new religion has swept the world—especially North America. We named it after ourselves, Secular *Humanism*. This false god and unholy religion wants us to believe that humans are preeminent and that all values should align to promote human happiness.

C.S. Lewis said, *"If you read history you will find that the Christians who did most for the present world were precisely those who thought most of the next. It is since Christians have largely ceased to think of the other world that they have become so ineffective in this."*

We must renounce humanism in all its forms. I exist to be loved by God, to love Him with all I am and to serve His Purpose and Design. It's just not about us! It is not about my personal happiness and success. This is about Jesus receiving the rewards of His suffering and about establishing His Kingdom in the earth realm. And, in this, I find immeasurable joy and happiness.

Three years ago Holy Spirit said to me, "There is no failure in the Kingdom." I was all over that. Then He spoke again, "There is no personal success in the Kingdom either." My reaction to this was a little flat to say the least. Oh, man, I had spent forty plus years being goal and success oriented. Even the Word says 'He will give me good success.' I must have heard wrong. "Holy Spirit?"

Holy Spirit explained that success in the Kingdom is the King's. As He makes us succeed at our ministries and Kingdom initiatives He shares the successes and celebrations with us. He *rewards* those who diligently seek Him. So the whole Kingdom system of success and reward is a unified system. He wins and we all win since we are all *in Him* and *He is our Reality*. And as the kingdoms of this world become the Kingdoms of Our Lord everyone wins!

Pssst! Can we talk about Destiny for a minute?

Your destiny is *not* your role or title; it is not what you **do** in the Kingdom. If it is you are a tool. Your destiny is *not to become a title*. You are not striving or contending *to be* an apostle, prophet, evangelist, pastor, or teacher. Your destiny does not manifest in the conferring of a title. This is an earth-bound, religious mindset that is frustrating the church.

Somehow we took what Paul meant to express as **functions** and elevated them to hierarchical titles. We should use titles to acknowledge function and of course to be honoring, but never was one five-fold function elevated over the others. A few months ago Holy Spirit told my friend and I that "…*form follows function*." That is a design and architectural adage that expresses that a thing should assume shape or form according to its intended function and use.

Then, the Lord showed us that the Body of Christ is intended to be alive and organic and growing! It is intended to look like—or be *parabolic of* a vineyard or grapevine, rather than an organizational chart or a building of bricks and mortar.

A vine grows rapidly and is not hindered by anything. It will grow up over a rock; it will bend around a tree. It can assume a new form at any time to continue to grow and perform its function which is bearing fruit. It is flexible and responsive to its environment. An inorganic building or a flow chart is not a fitting *parable* of the living Body of Christ because it is limited, rigid, unbending, and static.

Sometimes, in order to continue our function, or even to assume a new function and responsibility God will change our individual and corporate form. He will stretch us and bend us to suit His purpose in a certain season. If we cannot bend to His will we will break to His will. To stay changeable and resilient it will be far easier for us to relate to Him and to one another as we are called to *function in this season* rather than in hard and rigid roles and titles.

Corollary Destiny

OK, here is the very encouraging thing that the Lord showed me about *destiny…*

I was out in the woods with the Lord and the dog. Well, now is as good a time as any to confess; I have become a bit of a 'Jane the Baptist' over the past several years. I haven't eaten any bugs or anything…

One day a pastor friend called. Another friend of ours had called him to interpret a dream that he had about me.

My friend dreamt that he saw me out in the forest with the Lord, walking and talking. There were other people but they did not join in with me and the Lord. In the dream, John joins us and walks along. Funny thing is that I was wearing a fur. I told the guys, "That is not so remarkable, my friend's prophetic gift is very keen, I have not shaved my legs this week! Anyway…that was the day the Lord instructed me on **corollary destiny.**

It was in that season that I was really dying. I was happily dying! I wasn't actively ill and it was not suicide—this was *good death.* Do you know what I mean? It is displacement. Get 'me' out of here and good and dead and more of Christ comes to live in me. Paul said, "For to me to live [is] Christ, and to die [is] gain." (Philippians 1:21) I looked up the Greek word for "die" and one of its meanings is the death a seed goes through as it dies to become something else.

There are days when I feel less than the fullness of the Presence of God, and that provokes me to look at myself and my life and to seek more death. I ask God to point out what about me has to perish and then He debrides the old dead flesh. Then I enter a new realm of life! I enter into a greater revelation of *Christ as Reality*. That which is eternal cannot die. The Lord has taught me that since He defeated death, it is no longer a threat to those *in Christ Jesus!* Therefore death must benefit me. Even death must bless me! Ha!

"And we know that all things work together for good to them that love God, to them who are the called according to [his] purpose.
Romans 8:28

Amey Elizabeth died fourteen years ago. She is my daughter. Her name means "Beloved, Consecrated to God." She passed from my womb into eternity, into the open arms of God. She is not dead; she is just not *here.* She is one hundred percent in the heavenly realm. I am *in Christ Jesus,* the nexus of the physical and the heavenly, in both places at once. The Lord showed me one day at His sovereign invitation that Amey intercedes for our family and our ministry all of the time! Her life in Christ was set aside—*consecrated* to pray on behalf of the King and His Kingdom.

Many people asked me "Why?" "Why did Amey die?"

The week it happened I was barraged with that question. And in a moment of silence and great clarity I could see God. All I could see was God. And I could see a huge door open to me. In this time of great pain I saw the Door to the Throne Room of the Almighty open to me. And in that moment, I made one of the best decisions I ever made. *I looked up!*

And all I could see was the Father on His Throne surrounded by a rainbow of lights that were all of the colors of love. And so I passed through that door and I just stood there.

Father said nothing. I said nothing, I just stood there. His Presence was everything!

I began to feel that He expected something from me, that the invitation that I answered was to come and give Him something.

Knowing dawned within my spirit. This was one of the greatest opportunities that I will ever be presented with. I could feel that quite a lot of things in my life and future hinged on this one eternal moment. This was a moment of choice for me that would impact me for ever and impact many others.

A large and gentle angel approached me. I will never forget his face. His eyes were overflowing with tears and compassion. He looked at me as if to ask permission. I looked back at him and I said, "Yes." The angel took his hand out from under his wing and placed it above my ribs. He looked at me again with a teary smile. I heard myself say "Yes," again.

The angel put his hand inside my spirit and my chest at the same time. I felt no pain at all. He slowly removed his arm and hand from me and then he swaddled what he had removed. He held it so gently in his arms like it was the most precious and delicate thing he had ever touched. As he turned to take this precious parcel and present it before the Throne, he turned to me and looked at me again.

He laid the white swaddled parcel in the lap of the Father. Father took it up in His arms and unwrapped it. Though I could not see His face, I could hear his cry. He cried. He cried hard. But He was crying because He was pleased. I could feel that I was leaving soon. I turned to look at him once more and He had lifted His arms as if He were releasing a dove and I saw the word "WHY" floating up and away from Him and in the presence of His Holiness it disintegrated.

I gave Him **WHY**; He had already given me everything.

The only thing that died that day was the one thing that was strategized to kill my Kingdom destiny in Christ. The choice was clearly delineated: seek "Why" for all of my earthly days or seek HIM and His Kingdom all my days. He makes this easy. His grace is amazing.

Dear reader, if you have a "WHY", a "WHY NOT," a "WHY ME," a penchant for some *explanation*, I urge you in the name of Jesus the Christ to release it now and move into the **corollary destiny** He has prepared for you. The key to your Kingdom future is not in the "Why" and it is not in the answer, understanding, or information. Jesus is the Key. He is the Door. He is the Way, the Truth and the Life. No answer or explanation has any power to create the Kingdom and to produce Kingdom fruit!

Corollary Destiny is the term the Lord gave me to denote my own earthly destiny, so feel free to adopt the term. If I do not lay down my life for His, thereby aligning with His Destiny and Purpose, I can believe I have a destiny but it is not eternal and basically it is just a string of events within time and space that do not extend into eternity. That may be a good working definition of futility. No thanks.

However when I choose to enter into *Christ as Reality,* living in Him and giving my life over to Him, I parabolically align my life to His. He is the eternal director of my life and like the mathematical parabola I cling tightly to the curves. I have now entered into sharing His Destiny. His interests come first and we co-labor to establish *on earth as it is in heaven.* All of the rewards are His. He *is* my reward!

> *"But seek ye first the kingdom of God, and his righteousness;*
> *and all these things shall be added unto you."*
> Matthew 6:33

Put His Kingdom first and the stuff will show up. Well, actually, the Greek says that if you put the Kingdom first, you will be *increased.* One of the greatest aspects of this increase is the increased revelation of Jesus. There is nothing else. When the Kingdom of Jesus is our focus and our intention and our destination we have a guarantee that all that we need will be added and increased in our lives.

This just gets better and better! We all hope for *Thy Kingdom come, Thy will be done on earth as it is in heaven.* We all desire that the Lord receive all of the rewards of His suffering. We have hope for the day that the kingdoms of this world are the Kingdoms of our Lord. This is established! Our hope is our **proof.**

Our proof exists within our spirits as **faith.** This is the evidence of the *established fact.*

"If A, then B, therefore C." It is logic. And that is not to say that it is merely a mental construct, oh no. The Greek word *logic* actually means "*the word!*" I love that! Jesus, the *logos* word; *He IS logic.* Logic in the original language also means that which was *spoken. He IS the RHEMA!* This logic is very important stuff. Math is based upon logic and law is based upon logical precepts. Logic is the language of computer science. He is everywhere and All in All.

"Now faith is the substance of things hoped for, the evidence of things not seen. For by it the elders obtained a good report."
Hebrews 11:1-2

Here is my first valiant attempt to write a **theorem** of logic:

If **A** I have faith that I am in Christ and that I am called to co-labor with Him.

And **B** I hope for this, and haven't seen the physical realm manifestation…

Therefore: **C** My faith is the evidence of the coming good report.

There would be no faith resident in me if God had not planned the good report and the victorious outcome for me to participate in.

A **theorem** is a statement that can be demonstrated to be true by accepted mathematical operations and cases of logic. A theorem is the embodiment of a *general principle of truth*. So, nothing false can be called a theorem though it could be called a theory. A correct ***theorem*** is called a ***proof.***

A **corollary** is a fact that follows an already proven theorem, since the theorem is true and proven, no proof is required. A **corollary** is the *natural consequence, effect, or result* of the already proven theorem. The word origin for 'corollary' is Middle English and it means, "money paid for a garland." A garland was a token bestowed upon one who was victorious. *In Christ as Reality* you and I operate in and enact a ***Corollary Destiny to Christ's.***

Since it is not you or I that live but it is Christ Who lives we do not have to prove anything. **Our corollary destinies are a foregone conclusion!** This is because Jesus, The Resurrected One sits victoriously at the right hand of the Father. His divine destiny has been established of old. He *paid the price* at Calvary for all of our sins and so that we may have abundant life. He paid the price for our victorious lives! He is Truth and He is the Proof that our lives have ***eternal significance!***

You will walk in the destiny He has for you. It is the earnest of your inheritance as His child. If you live a parabolic life, achieving your corollary destiny is a done deal.

FOCUS

We have to remember that we are all together and unified in Christ. We must never forget that the desired **goal**, **outcome** and **destiny** is one: ***that Jesus Christ receives the rewards of His sufferings, that it be on earth as it is in heaven, and that*** *every knee bow and every tongue confess that He is Lord to the glory of God the Father!* There is no other goal.

We can say that the goal of the church is to evangelize, and so it is, however we have to view evangelism in light of Jesus receiving the glory He is due. People are saved *for Jesus* and that also means they do not perish in hell. We can say that the goal of the church is the ministry of Isaiah 61 and Isaiah 58, and so it is, so that all men will experience the love and redemptive power of Christ and thereby He receives the rewards of His sufferings. No way is this about us. We are created for Him in order to worship Him.

Oh, Father, grant us the great grace to refocus. We have been looking out of the wrong end of the scope and we need a redeemed perspective.

Dave and I had our house open on Monday nights for apostolic prayer. This is praying the heart of the Father and the prayers of the apostles to establish His will and Kingdom in the earth. This is prayer that is for Him, about Him, and led by Him. Most Mondays after we finished our apostolic prayer time the Lord would welcome us to bring requests for healing before Him. Even then, we waited on Him to invite since these nights were all about Him.

As time went on our group became more and more chatty. People would talk about who was sick and needed prayer, who was preaching what where and so on. It was becoming another social time and time of *ministry to the Christians* rather than doing what He had asked us to do, pray His heart.

Wanting to be polite we didn't say much. We would gently try to refocus the group but they weren't having it. Finally the stuff hit the fan one night when the group began, and I wish I was exaggerating, discussing the *ills of society* and what we, the church should do about them. I stepped into the kitchen to pull myself together. I asked the Lord to grace me to regroup. He just let my simmer hit a boil. My heart thudded and pounded in my chest and I walked back into the prayer room in the red zone. I murmured to myself under my breath, "shut up, shut up, shut up."

I opened my mouth and heard myself let out a torrent. I demanded to know how this group went from being focused on the Lord to being focused on the ills of society. I demanded to know how the church could have any positive affect on society when we couldn't focus on God for two hours once a week. I went into a low orbit around the earth and splash landed in my swimming pool hours later after everyone had gone home!

That's not polite. I am aware of that. Sometimes I think polite is the mantra of a controlling spirit. We get the fire of God in our bellies and we are ready to release His fire into the earth and a nagging little voice whispers, "That would not be polite." There are times when we either obey God or be polite and the two choices exclude one another.

Focusing on Him is an imperative!

In this season of harvest anything else is fatal. Or crazy. Whichever is more polite. We will arrive at the point we focus upon. We will become what we behold. A brother just released a prophetic word with the illustration that race drivers are told to never focus on the wall as they are speeding through the turns on the racetrack. They are trained to focus on the open road ahead and aim for it. We need to focus on Jesus and aim to be more Christ-like. This is what creation yearns for, people who embody the virtues of the Christ and who are the gates of heaven!

The open road ahead of us had better be Jesus and the Kingdom of Jesus Christ come to earth! This has to be our aim and focus. If He is not our focus we will end up somewhere else, perhaps a false religious realm full of platitudes but without power. As we have agreed, *"Don't go there!"*

We focus first with our hearts. What is the intention of our heart? What ever it is we will end up there! If the focus of our heart is *seeking first the Kingdom of God* then everything else that we do and say will align with that focus. Then, *all these things will be added unto you.* I really believe that 'all these things' is the enormous category that everything other than the Kingdom objective goes into. 'All these things' are lesser things when prioritized with establishing the Kingdom of Jesus and securing His reward.

We must focus from heaven to earth. We need to focus from the vantage point of heaven. This is the place of the divine directive. Heaven must be the home of our hearts, and we must aim all of our heavenly-birthed intentions into the earth realm. We aim our hearts and our intentions from heaven into the earth because the lighting is much better in heaven. What I mean to say is that in the heavenly realm we are able to see with the eyes of our hearts and we have supernatural vision.

If we focus on the earth realm from the earth realm we will surely miss. Here, we see through a glass darkly. The physical realm is a shadow land. Earth-bound perceptions are flawed and influenced by those who are not God. This is as dangerous as going quail hunting with Dick Cheney. There is too much chance of getting hit by friendly fire. Too many casualties of war. Let's aim from heaven into the earth to establish heaven here and get it right. Hit the target. We shoot, aim, and then look around to see that people got hurt by man-made plans and programs. Our best bet is to not make plans and not establish goals that are not congruent to His Kingdom plans.

Scene in Heaven

God calls up a preacher to check in with him and see how everything is going. The preacher says, "Hey, God, so glad you called. I have been meaning to call you, by the way. I am working up plans for building a new sanctuary—state of the art!" God says, "You made plans? Well cancel them. We are building a Kingdom here!"

If it's not in heaven we don't need it here, it is refuse. It is extraneous and it becomes a weight and a fetter. This is the stuff we are called to lay aside. Maybe we should begin seeing things as "Kingdom things" and "lesser things."

No matter how good an idea is it will not produce the fruit of the Kingdom unless it is birthed in heaven. If it is not fertilized by the *sperma* seed of God then it is not His baby and will turn out to be illegitimate. We cannot afford to go on wasting Kingdom resources, and we have to wake up to the fact that God provides for His own and does not feel obligated to maintain that which He did not issue.

Will you have grace for me? This word has been germinating in me at least three years!

You and I dear child of God are called to **be resources**. You are a **resource of heaven** and one of limitless supply at that. Be fruitful and multiply. Bear abundant fruit. We have all encountered folks who have been in the church their entire lives and are still in consumption mode. Many times these precious ones can become a distraction to you and your ministry due to their constant demand for personal ministry. This can be exhausting and wearying. Our newest grandson, Braden is eleven weeks old. (Officially he is the cutest baby ever!) Braden had a little bit of colic there for a while and got a bit out of whack. Our daughter, Heidi had to nurse the little guy every hour on the hour! She became totally exhausted!

The same is true for folks who never move from milk to meat, they are so demanding that those in relationship with them are weary.

"For when for the time ye ought to be teachers, ye have need that one teach you again which [be] the first principles of the oracles of God; and are become such as have need of milk, and not of strong meat."
Hebrews 5:12

Maybe the most gracious and loving thing to do is to **encourage growth**. Perhaps we should prophesy life and fruit and meat and stop suckling.

Again, this is the day in which we need to **focus on heaven and the harvest** and not on enabling others to stay on the milk. Having said this I realize that discipling is a very important ministry in the church. This is to be a process of maturation and multiplication.

Focus With Prophetic Vision to See Destiny

In this current season it is imperative to *see with prophetic vision*. Remain focused like a laser beam on Him. We need to *hear with the ears of our spirits*. We need to have our senses exercised and our members so submitted to Him that He can turn us on a dime. We have all noticed an ***acceleration*** coming. Common sense tells us that as everything in the earth realm speeds up we need to increase the pace at which we can change and embrace the new things He is doing!

I was in an intercessory prayer meeting a few years ago and I should have stayed home. I had spent a great day with the Lord, and I had the fire of God on me. So, needless to say, I went into the meeting 'fired up.' Like I said, I should have stayed home and tended the embers. A man in the group was praying for our church. He was asking God to have patience with us because we were like a big ocean liner and we were slow in the turns. He was asking God to have understanding and compassion on us for being ungainly and difficult to steer. *He was asking God to adapt to our unresponsiveness.*

I had been praying on the floor, face down. I lifted my head and began to yell: "Take your hands off the wheel! Hands off the wheel! Abandon ship! Abandon ship!" I *think* I was interceding, I really do. I think I would rather experience the shipwreck like Paul and friends in Acts 27 and 28 than to be a hostage on a big old clunker of a vessel that is a slow boat to nowhere. God demonstrated signs and wonders through Paul after the "Minnow" was lost and smashed to smithereens. God knew that a storm was coming and Paul warned the captain and crew. Still, God did not perform a miracle on the ship. It was a man-made construct and a human idea. God implements His own ideas.

So it is with our destinies. Whatever our idea or concept of our destiny is, God's is much greater and infinitely more satisfying. I believe that we all share One Destiny—His! We are all one in *Christ as Reality.* We live and move and have our beings in Him, so *we have already arrived in our Destiny.* You are in your destiny right now! There may be events and fruit that are in the process of manifestation, but here and now, if you are *in Christ,* you have arrived. Our destination is to be in Christ Jesus and He is the Way into that Destiny. He is All in All and all there is to be desired. He calls us His Own. Where do we go from there? Only deeper into the vastness of Him.

He is Destiny. Paul says it best:

"For I determined not to know any thing among you, save Jesus Christ, and him crucified."
1 Corinthians 2:2

If titles and roles reflect more about us than about Christ then maybe they are a veil and a hindrance. If we tout our own destinies more than we reflect the Love of God and His Ultimate Purpose, we are off *par*, meaning we are no longer aligned to His Destiny. Our lives are not *parabolic* of heaven or of Christ.

When we are focused *on Him,* with a *heavenly perspective,* and *He is our Destiny,* then we have come into parity and alignment with heaven. Release the Glory of the Lord.

"And these signs shall follow them that believe; In my name shall they cast out devils; they shall speak with new tongues; They shall take up serpents; and if they drink any deadly thing, it shall not hurt them; they shall lay hands on the sick, and they shall recover."
Mark 16:17-18

CHAPTER ELEVEN

THE ELEVENTH DIMENSION

I believe we are all together in His Spirit and we are arriving in a place of summing up all of this prophetic exhortation. We are converging in the eleventh dimension.

The *"Unified Theory of Everything"* was a holy grail to every scientist and quantum theorist since Einstein. Physicists, mathematicians and theorists want to find a theory to unify the cosmos and the quantum field. Einstein spent several decades in pursuit of this theory. It was the 'lion' that he chased. He wanted to establish a theory that would unite all the forces of the universe into one elegant and precise equation. He wanted to see this explanation of everything laid out in a one inch mathematical expression.

But, Einstein had eyes to see! He had a *parabolic vision* of the elusive Everything Theory:

"Nature shows us only the tail of the lion. But, I do not doubt that the lion belongs to it even though he cannot at once reveal himself because of his enormous size."

Einstein said:

*Behind every great theory there is a simple physical picture that
even lay people can understand.
If a theory does not have a simple underlying picture, then the
theory is probably worthless.*
The important thing is the physical picture;
math is nothing but bookkeeping."

Einstein, you are the original *'parabola man.'* You are hugging the curves.

Einstein appreciated the power of **vision**. He knew that the facts and theories that science uncovers are pre-existent in the realm of *vision*. He had eyes to see. He had a keen appreciation for the visionary and in fact he asserted that the visionary had preeminence over that which can be explained on paper.

"Einstein's Lion", his analogy for the illusive theory that he sought, is rather like First Corinthians 13:9 *"For we know in part and we prophesy in part."* The Theory of Relativity was Einstein holding the tail of the lion. This he and his fellows had a grip on, yet there was more that was *unseen*. I love that Einstein believed and trusted the *unseen*. He knew that the rest of the lion existed because he had a firm grasp on the tail.

I wonder if he had an inkling that the tail of the lion he held was attached to the Lion of the Tribe of Judah!

After the death of Einstein many physicists and quantum theorists forged on in the quest for their holy grail, this elusive *Theory of Everything*. This theorem had to explain and demonstrate cosmology, including the creation of the universe and the entire visible universe, and it had to explain and demonstrate the quantum unseen realm. Could it be that one theorem and equation could express both? Was there a theorem so perfect that it would bridge this gap?

A school of physicists arose out of this quest. They gave birth to *String Theory,* and as is the case with everything that we have seen going on in this realm of science, String Theory brought with it an *added dimension!*

The idea behind String Theory is that the universe is made up of vibrating strings. These strings vibrate at specific resonant frequencies. Think of the strings of a violin. Different particles have differing properties and therefore they vibrate at various frequencies. There were five separate String Theories that up until recently were considered complementary yet disparate.

Strangely, the five proven and solid, yet separate String Theories remind me of the current state of the five-fold Christian ministries; apostolic, prophetic, evangelical, pastoral, teaching. They are all essential, they are all profoundly necessary, yet they are parallel and disconnected in many ways. We do not seem to be renewing and reforming within current structures and mindsets. What the manifold ministries need is a *unifying convergence*—a point of *singularity.* I believe with all of my being that this place of unity is called *in Christ Jesus.* We must wake up and find ourselves all together in one accord—in *autos*—in *Him.* This is the hope of the ages. This is what the whole of creation yearns for!

You will agree with heaven and I will agree with you *and* heaven and we'll put ten thousand to flight! Many more will join in and we, the Body of Christ, will *take Dominion of the planet and establish on earth as it is in heaven!* OK? We will see the Lord Jesus high and lifted up and we will see his Glory cover the earth as the waters cover the seas!

Seeing All That is There

Remember the quantum stuff that is simultaneously in two places at one time? String Theory very effectively demonstrates how a particle can appear as a point and as a line or string at the same time. Viewed from one dimension, the particle appears as a string because we see the dimension of length. From another dimension, the particle is a singular point because we do not see its dimensionality. I believe that may be how it is as we attempt to look into the spiritual realm from the material realm. We do not actually perceive all that we are seeing because *we are unaccustomed to the added dimensions.* However when we *see in the spirit,* meaning that we look at spirit with spiritual eyes, we see the manifold nature of the heavenly realm. The other dimensions unfold before us.

How can it be that the spirit realm is all around us and many are unable to have the slightest perception of it? I believe the spirit of religion has blinded us to the reality of the realm of God's Spirit and the fact that we are preeminently spirit. Doctrine has darkened our eyes and now many only see the familiar shadow land of acceptable Christian fable. In other words, if you have not been taught that you are *allowed to see* into the dimension of spirit, you will not even entertain the possibility of seeing that dimension, let alone living there. Conversely, if you have been taught that to see in the spiritual dimension is wrong or just for the New Agers, then chances are not good for having any vision at all.

There is a story of some contemporary anthropologists who visited a very remote island inhabited by a native people who had never had any contact whatsoever with the civilized world or any other peoples. The scientists were the first to ever make contact with these people. One day a pair of large sailing ships appeared on the horizon as the scientists were on the beach meeting with the tribal leaders. The scientists got excited and edged closer to observe. They waved "hi" and jumped up and down. The natives looked at the scientists as if they were nuts. Despite all attempts to point out the ships, they went unseen by the natives.

This led the anthropologists to conduct an entirely new study of the phenomenon they had just witnessed. Experiments concluded that the native people were entirely *unable to see* the large vessels. The natives were blind to the ships. Not until the natives first learned the *concept* of "ship" did they actually have the physical ability to see the ships.

Because "ship" was off the grid for the natives "ship" did not exist and was not a part of the reality they experienced.

What are we missing as a result of our narrowly plotted grid?
Father, forgive us! **Friends, we have to give God permission**
to mess with our reality!

Lord I do not want to miss anything You have for me—regardless of how 'out there' it may be! You have my permission to bring me into any and all revelation that you may have for me personally or corporately. Jesus, take me with You –off the map and off the grid!

M-Theory/Mem Theory

In the pursuit of their all inclusive theory, the quantum theorists found that either they were stretching known reality and the universe, or it was expanding on its own. As the research progressed, *more and more dimensions were revealed.* As one theorem was proven it pointed to yet another which was the mathematical expression of *yet another dimension.*

It is at this point in the history of the quest for the Theory that *convergence* manifests!

As the physicists walked further and further off the map something amazing occurred: the five disparate String Theories *converged in a higher dimension.* In this **eleventh dimension** all of the five String Theories proved to be TRUE.

In the *Eleventh Dimension,* all of the five string theories, general relativity, and quantum mechanics knit together forming a *web of relationships.* This relational web which occurs "looks" mathematically and theoretically like a *membrane* as it is 'viewed' from the perspective of the eleventh dimension. Hence, this theory is called "M" theory for membrane. Out of this has developed a new protoscience called brane cosmology. In this view of the universe, our visible, knowable universe is contained within these membranes and thought to exist *inside a higher dimensional space.*

Hello, earth to the scientists: We could have told you that. Could it be that this *higher dimensional space* is our higher reality we know as *in Christ Jesus?*

"For by him were all things created, that are in heaven, and that are in earth, visible and invisible, whether [they be] thrones, or dominions, or principalities, or powers: all things were created by him, and for him:
And he is before all things, and by him all things consist."
Colossians 1:15-17

I remind you: I am a literal-minded person. I take God at His Word and I take all of scripture and all rhema Word *literally.* If the Word says that all things consist by Christ, well then by golly, all things have their consistence and existence by way of Him.

The Greek word for consist is *sunistao.* It means to be created and sustained by. It means to exist together and to be held together by. It also means to be comprised of, to be established, and to be united.

I truly believe that this is what Paul meant in saying that He is our All in All. This is what is meant by Acts 17:28, that in Him we live and move and have our being. He is He that Was and Is and Is to Come.

ho on kai ho en kai ho erchomenos

> "Holy, holy, holy, Lord God Almighty, which was,
> and is, and is to come."
> Rev. 4:8b

Mem Theory

Mem is the thirteenth letter in the Hebrew aleph-bet. It is pronounced like the English "m." The symbol for the letter mem is a pictogram of water. The gematric numeric value assigned to mem is forty. Prophetically, and as it relates to knowing the times and seasons, this is significant.

Mem also symbolizes one of the Names of God in Judaism. The symbol for mem stands for "Makom" God the Omnipresent. He is present everywhere, and *He is Everywhere.* He is the Lord "Ha-Makom" which means "the place" and "the omnipresence." In other words—*He is The Place.* He is our locality.

Hebrew mystics explained the quantum M-Theory many centuries ago. The rabbinical scholars got there first with their concept of *Tzimtzum.* Tzimtzum is the concept of contraction, constriction, and concealment. The words *world* and *concealment* come from the same Hebrew root word *olam.* It conveys that God created a conceptual space that emerged because He chose to conceal and constrict His infinite Self in that place. He did this to create a *conceptual space* in which His own infiniteness would not overwhelm everything. Essentially He created a finite and independent reality. In this place created beings can operate in free will.

This is also a place that is sort of separated from the direct Presence of God by a plenum or a membrane. To me, it is reminiscent of God revealing His Glory to Moses but putting His hand over the cleft of the rock in an act of concealment. In fact, God says to Abraham "there is a *place* by me I will put you there." This is the Hebrew Ha-Makom. Then He told Moses that He was going to cover him with His own hand as Moses stood on this rock. The original language here is so rich in meaning. God said to Moses—I have created a sure place for you and on this rock you will stand. I believe that is Christ the Rock and it is the earth, the third rock from the sun. God told Moses, "I will hedge you in with My own hand—the palm of My hand is your protection."

It is as if this place or tzimtzum is somehow contained making it a finite world that exists within the infinite. It is the physical within the metaphysical. This is uncannily like the M-Theory representations of the eleventh dimension which is the spatial home of all of the other dimensions.

The letter mem is represented by a water image. As I think of water and membranes the process of birth comes to mind. I believe that the Lord is pointing us to the facts that the membrane of the physical realm that has held back the birthing of the glorious church is about to burst forth as the water, The River of Holy Spirit, penetrates all. **He will pour out His Spirit on all flesh.**

"And it shall come to pass afterward, [that] I will pour out my spirit upon all flesh; and your sons and your daughters shall prophesy, your old men shall dream dreams, your young men shall see visions:"
Joel 2:28

This is so beyond all of my faculties that it stirs the spirit of the fear of the Lord in me! I hear Him calling to us and saying "Pay attention!" It feels like our plane is racing down the runway and we are all about to go for the spiritual flight of our lives, right into other dimensions. We are blessed to live in this time.

Above in Joel 2 the word says that it shall come to pass afterward. This is a phrase often used in scripture to indicate a formula of transition. It seems to indicate that a certain cycle has been completed and a new season is beginning. The former is passed and the new is being birthed.

These are precisely the prophetic attributes of the number 40. **Forty** is symbolic of the cloture of times of spiritual preparation and wilderness trials and seasons. Forty is frequently used to commemorate events in God's calendar. I pray that as the church we have come to the end of wandering in the wilderness of religion and that we are awakening to *Jesus Christ as Reality*.

In the beginning He, the Word, was with God and **He was God**. Then He created time and stepped into time through the womb of a willing virgin. He impacted time in a way that nothing else has ever been impacted because He split time in two. Now, as the Son of Man, existing inside of physical space and time, **He is.** And, in a relatively short time, **He is coming!** Once again we shall behold Him as He returns to earth, to space and time as we are currently experiencing it. It is the second coming of Christ.

Look at the impact of the first advent of Christ. The latter is greater than the former for we shall behold Him in all of His Glory. Our shadow land will be lit with the phosphorescent Light of Heaven Himself. Every knee shall bow and every tongue shall confess that Jesus Christ is Lord to the Glory of God the Father.

We are so on the verge of this!

Do you know what time it is?

I believe it is Eleven/Forty.

Do you know where you are?

I truly believe we need to be *in Christ Jesus, experiencing Him as our Reality*. We have to be in that *eleventh dimension*, seeing from a heavenly vantage point and perspective.

> *"And he carried me away in the spirit to a great and high mountain, and shewed me that great city, the holy Jerusalem, descending out of heaven from God,"*
> Revelation 21:12

Like John the Revelator, we need to allow ourselves to be carried away in the Spirit to the Mountain of God in order to see from His place of habitation and to share His perspective.

We need to be 'virgins of the eleventh hour' trimming our lamps and soaking in and soaking up the oil of His Presence. There is a midnight cry coming. The Lion of the Tribe of Judah has His head held high and He is preparing to release a roar that will break all barriers. I believe that presently it is the eleventh hour and our wanderings are over. We must now enter in.

Eleven: the Number of the Prophetic

Echad is the Hebrew word for the ordinal number eleven. It denotes 'eleventh' in a succession of numbers. It also means first in the sense of *forerunner, once and for all, certain, together, and one place*.

Eleven in scripture symbolizes the prophetic. It represents intuition, patience, sensitivity, courage, spirituality, and spiritual inheritance. When eleven occurs in scripture in terms of time, it is seen as a time of a new cycle, a new beginning and a paradigm shift. Eleven" was a time, a time period or a season for *power shifts.*

Eleven represents the time period just before Jesus' rule is established in the earth realm! It is no coincidence that science has discovered and mathematically demonstrated the *eleventh dimension* in this season and in this hour.

You know, when I was a kid growing up in 'church', the world was flat. Confidentially I tell you that because I knew the love of Jesus, I figured I could tolerate the banal existence 'church' represented to me until I died or Jesus came back. Thank You, Holy Spirit for personal and corporate revelation! This has to be the most exciting time to be alive. It is as if everything is coming together into a singularity and everything, and I mean everything, testifies of Jesus. Everything is revealing Jesus. He is making all things new.

The **Eleventh Dimension** is a prophetic time and it is a real place in the dimension of the Spirit. It is a *convergence* of time and place that is *in Christ Jesus.* At this critical juncture, we must be *prophetic people.* We must have eyes to see and ears to hear. The Spirit is speaking to the churches. He is speaking to you. There is an invitation open to each of us to 'come up here' into the heavenly realm and into the eleventh dimension to receive revelation of heaven and of Jesus.

The material realm is speaking and revealing Christ. Again, we must have *parabolic* mindsets to perceive all that is being revealed. If we observe all of existence in a *parabolic sense,* we will open to instruction and revelation. Did you know that there are *eleven parables* that Jesus spoke? These are His word-pictures spoken into the earth realm to give us a glimpse of *as it is in heaven.* He told us these things so that we could use the dominion and authority He gave us to implement heaven in the earth! The Kingdom of heaven is at hand! The Kingdom of heaven is within you. It is not just the idea or notion of heaven, it is the dimension of heaven that is in each of us because we are filled with Holy Spirit and we are *in Christ Jesus.*

This is REALITY. It is not a fable. It is not a far off promise. It is revelation of Christ that we must embrace and that we must embody. All of creation yearns for the manifestation of the sons of God. We cannot be His children if we do not carry a part of Him. Jesus has brought us into His family and we have been given divine DNA. It is eleven o'clock and it is now the time and season for us to come forth.

We must embrace our heritage as a prophetic people who will cry out, "Prepare ye the way of the Lord!" We must decree heaven and the second advent of Christ into the earth realm.

Jesus appeared *eleven times* between His resurrection and His ascension. He is appearing to you in manifold ways. Perceive it! Then, decree and declare the revelation to all. The heavens and the earth declare Him and His majesty. All of creation sings his praise. Realign your concept of reality to perceive the parabolic in all of life.

What is life?

It's Parabolic!

Scientifically speaking, a *parabola* is an expression of all of the points that are equidistant from a line. It is a set of *points of agreement*. It has a *Director*—a never-ending line which is the *focus*.

You are a beautiful, **parabolic expression** of Christ-likeness.

Jesus is the **Director** of our lives. He is constant, fixed, never-ending, eternal.

He is our **focus.**

"One thing have I desired of the LORD, that will I seek after; that I may dwell in the house of the LORD all the days of my life, to behold the beauty of the LORD, and to enquire in his temple."
Psalm 27:4

We must focus on Him for our lives to line up and be in agreement with Him.

"Let it be on earth as it is in heaven."

Our *Reality* can be Parabolic and aligned with heaven. It will be the glorious experience of *Jesus Christ as Reality* when our singular focus is the Lord of heaven and earth and when our intentions align with His. This will manifest as we live to "seek ye first the Kingdom of God and His righteousness." Then, our realities are *prophetic and full of revelation.*

Now, go. Explore the glorious reality of a parabolic, prophetic life of intimacy with the Lover of Your Soul!

August 12, 2008

This is a prophetic post script, spoken to me by a very sober and serious Holy Spirit.

Beloveds, this is it, this *IS* the jumping-off point and the edge of the proverbial cliff. We must see ourselves as the church in *'shift or become irrelevant mode.'*

This is not in any way a prophetic encouragement to shift into some kind of emotional high gear, or charismatic frenzy. Quite the opposite! This is a prophetic exhortation to all of us to shift and shift *immediately* into the parabolic paradigm that *Jesus Christ is Our Reality,* and no lesser reality can be trusted—no matter how much it looks like church, religion, revival, or a former thing.

You see, the danger is not in becoming irrelevant to seekers, the unsaved, converts, Christians, or society, *the imminent danger is in becoming irrelevant to Jesus!*

(It is not like we haven't been warned by John the Beloved in Revelation 3.)

These are crazy, perhaps perilous times in which people are tempted to hold on to or grab hold of *something.* No 'thing' will preserve us to the day of our redemption— *only Jesus!*

We must embrace only the authentic Jesus and become like Him.

No lesser things!

We must be balanced in the operation of Grace, and we must be entirely committed to wait upon Him and the moves of Holy Spirit that He initiates. In this time of waiting on Him may we all have the grace and discernment to disregard any lesser things.

The cry in my heart is this:

"The only hope I have of being an authentic Christian is to only embrace the authentic Jesus."

May Jesus Christ alone be your Reality,
Kelly Deppen

3189681

Made in the USA